Praise for *Right W*

"Reading *Right Wrong Night Song* is like sitting down with an old friend you haven't seen in years and realizing that there is a current, a life force, at work on the page. It is a recognizable humanity that finds its voice in these poems. The variations in tone—heartfelt, wise, at times even silly—celebrate the uneasy truce with the natural world that needs to be brokered in order to survive at the edge of the continent where the very name beyond the ocean's shore is a paradox: *peace*. But how peaceful is it? California, where tectonic plates can erupt and scrape at any time. Small dogs can be carried away by hungry predators when your back has turned. And sudden beauty—like watching your spouse asleep on a sofa in front of the TV or discovering family among strangers such as yourself—can be found in such lovely songs indeed."

—**Laurel Ann Bogen**
Author of *Psychosis in the Produce Department* (Red Hen Press)

"In *Right Wrong Night Song*, Jeff Rogers sifts through his recollections and observations. He bears witness but also pushes beyond the moment and wonders if there's more. At his insistence, "We cast our imagination out past the limits of our senses" and reel in more than just what we think we know. We net clusters of memories both precious and prescient, some so small we might miss them slipping from our grasp and some so big they might topple us. We chum the water for times such as these just to glimpse a flash of something bright and urgent rippling just below, praying we'll be around when it breaks the surface on its own. And sometimes we snag our hooks on something deeper within ourselves, deeper than we intended to go, and wonder if this will be the thing that pulls us under. Rogers serves us a haunting and tender collection of poems that beg us to question what we know and what we see."

—**bridgette bianca**
Author of *be/trouble* (Writ Large Projects)

World Stage Press
Verse from the Village

RIGHT WRONG NIGHT SONG

RIGHT WRONG NIGHT SONG

Jeff Rogers

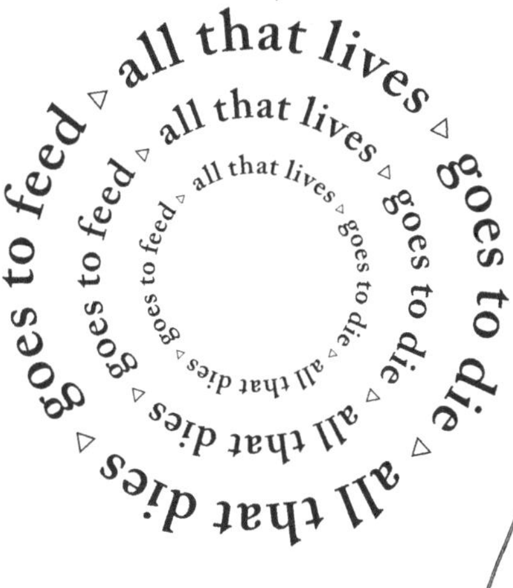

World Stage Press
Verse from the Village

Right Wrong Night Song

ISBN: 978-1-952952-47-0

First Edition, 2022

Printed in the United States of America

Cover Photograph by Jeff Rogers
Cover Design by Jeff Rogers and Emily Anne Evans
Layout Design by Emily Anne Evans

For my mother the archaeologist
who taught me that everyone who ever lived
was just as real as you and me
and that every day alive is an adventure
even the day of your own death.

Dr. Margaret (Peggy) Anne Bishop Rogers Holman
June 21, 1940 – April 18, 2006

For my father the political scientist
who taught me to recognize my biases
and that every day alive is a chance
to ask another question, to turn the world in your mind
and see it from a new point of view.

Dr. Chester (Chet) Benjamin Rogers
October 20, 1939 – September 26, 2020

With love and gratitude
from your wayward poet son.

Every life is a story. Every story craves an ending.

***

For my wife Elise Rodriguez
with all the love I have to give.

I can still see that exact smile
March 17, 1994
when I first saw you in the middle of your room.
As if through clear water I saw all the way down
and out through that moment
into our long shared future.

I would not be the writer or the man I am if not for you.
I owe you more than I can ever say
and love you more than a book of poems can express.

A FISH WITH FROG'S
EYES,
CREATION IS PERFECT

–Bob Kaufman, "The Poet"

Oh, the kind of angel I'm on the side of
Won't ever try to hide from the terrible responsibilities of love!

–Kenneth Patchen, "Because Everybody Looked So Friendly I Ran"

It's hard to be a human.

–Peggy Holman

Contents

III. EVERYTHING ALIVE MOVING

Preface: The Splendor of Our Finite

Time can be measured objectively: seconds, minutes, hours.

But our perception of time is subjective, emotional. Can we measure that? I believe we do, intuitively.

I consider the moment to be the fundamental unit of measurement for human time.

We know when we've had a moment. We can talk to each other about moments and we all know what we mean. The moment is common currency in a universal tongue.

There are other things we can say about moments.

First of all, because each of us is genetically unique and all the circumstances of our birth and experiences following are particular to us, my moments will never be the same as your moments—even if the moment is shared. Even if I were saying these words to you across a table or walking together on a beach, your experience of the moment would be different from my experience of the same moment. You have your unique moments and I mine.

Time for each of us can flow, stutter, stagger, or skip like a stone across a lake. For me right now time might be flying while for you it only drags. We each occupy a one-person time zone.

And because we live in time—forced residents of the fourth dimension—time moves for us in only one direction: relentlessly forward. We can move around with relative freedom in the other three dimensions, but not in that sticky fourth.

So only you ever get your moments and you only ever get them once.

Our lives are a succession of moments that can never be repeated. Take this moment right now in its fullness—survey each of your senses in turn. How many sounds can you hear right now? Voices, an airplane out the window, an annoying electronic beep somewhere. Notice all the sights available to your eyes: faces, colors, shapes, motion through air. What tastes sit on your tongue? What scents rise to your nostrils on the in-breath? Those thoughts and emotions that flit through your brain. It might be impossible to attend to it all, put it all together, fully experience any given moment in the round in all six senses.

Yet once this moment is gone it will never come back. Where does it go?

There is beauty and terror in that. Crushing sadness. Searing joy.

All there in our moments.

That's what a life is.

We grace the infinite with the splendor of our finite.

I believe that poems can capture and hold pieces of our moments, sing them back into a second life.

For me, that's part of what poetry is—an effort to live in my moments, find things in my moments that can be shared. To eff the ineffable. To find things in your moments for you that can be called back, experienced anew, reflected upon, captured, shared.

Each moment will elude us.
Each moment ripped away on the wind.

Each moment is all that is promised us.
Each moment whipped away on the wind.

Each moment whipped away on the wind.

RIGHT
WRONG
NIGHT
SONG

all that lives
goes to die
all that dies
goes to feed
all that lives

I.

WHAT GROWS BELOW GROUND

Headstrong Weed

If I
could just find
one crack
in that wall
to push through

My voice
like a tuft
of wild grass

My voice
like a headstrong weed

What Grows Below Ground

In tribute to artist and master printer Richard Duardo

That which casts out, escapes from under
The garden wall, groping blind for lands beyond.
Taproot that pushes down through seed-ground seeking source.
A time traveler of sorts, arrow tendril pointing all the way back
To that very moment when the big bang
Snapped the whole universe inside out.
That ecstasy of first creation when it explodes its banks,
From ecstatic trances of the first cave painters
Facing their rock walls rolling and swimming in firelight,
On down to us, standing here, feeling nearly deaf,
Nearly blind, and nearly mute, brushes in hand
Before the empty canvas, or fingers poised above keys
Before the blank blinking screen, our arts
The coded thoughts of the universe passed through
Our twining neurons and into our hands,
Into those frames on the walls before us,
Into our poems clutched in shaking fingers,
With their stutter of language, words cobbled together
From such thin and rickety letters.
How that viny S, for instance, twirls up and around,
How that scaffold E makes a ladder of three rungs from earth up to sky,
And how that Y dips its shy tail into subterranean waters below,
Then spreads its naked arms in welcome
To the rain and the star showers above.

Rooms of C19

I remember early March
when the virus walked on my chest
walked my breath away
left me unsure where air began and where
the flat board that pressed my lungs
　　　　shallow.

But here I am. I woke up.
So what do I have to complain about
in this room crowded with dead?
Still, I remember that night
when I went to bed with a bad joke:
Well, hope I see you in the morning
and the modest fear of not waking
　　　　ever again.

With my wife two days behind
we cycled through symptoms: the fever
that boiled our brains, the limbs too heavy
to lift off the bed and carry across the floor.
We wondered through those first few
pandemic weeks of 2020 even
as the country wondered:
　　　　COVID-19?

Next door to the room of the dead
those like my wife, left wondering
how many pieces of themselves
Death stole away
before leaving them stranded
with fingers and toes of needle-numbed fire
and chunks of petrified lung,
heart-blood clotted,
vitality hollowed out,
winding roads to their summit torn away
and tumbled into their canyons,
internal bridges left crumbling,
　　　　collapsed.

In this room, survivors are left
to pick through their own rubble,
catalogue the pieces missing, the absences,
detect the hidden legacies—
the word you reach for and it's not there,
the gulp of air your lungs grab for
and come up empty,
the energy you try to summon
and fall short. And then what sticks to you,
the signs Death left behind
for you to find later, the trip wires,
little explosions lying in wait
so you'll never forget—
the trip to the ER two months after
to find hundreds of tiny blood clots
like buried landmines in your lungs,
the vessels inside somewhere inflamed,
swollen, bottlenecks that choke
the free flow of life's throb and pump,
electricity and elasticity of thought,
because your own defenses
turned against
          you.

That old abstract question
made immediate and concrete:
          Who am I
                    now?
          Who can I
                    still be?

Systemic Pandemic

July 4, 2020

It's COVID-19 Spring
and above my head
in a branch of the Chinese elm
fanned above my patio
two needle beaks
poke from a gray hummingbird nest
their every life taste in the air
days new
and what do they know
            of human
            pandemic?

It's BLM Summer
because Ahmaud Arbery
Breonna Taylor
George Floyd
will never taste life again.
People amass in the peaceful thousands
and a few scattered windows get smashed.
I stand in a gravel parking lot
in a small California town
on the Fourth of July
breathing my own stale air
in a black tube mask
when I see a hawk
glide above the street
and what does he know
            of systemic
            white human violence
            against Black human beings?

COVID & BLM Summer
orange man
yellow hair
white house
guarded on all sides by temperature guns

cotton swabs on blue plastic stems
shoved up nostrils and down throats.
Helicopter blades thump the air,
drown out the voices he won't hear:
spiky voices speaking virus,
moans of the dying,
cries for the dead,
gasps that claw at last breath
against lungs full of white ice
against white knee on Black neck
against cooed comfort from the nurse
whose gloved hand holds the bare hand
of her patient as he dies
and only her eyes show
the final gift of her smile
behind surgical mask
under N95
under face shield
standing in for his wife—
witness behind cell phone glass.

Orange man yellow hair white house
shields himself with an upside-down Bible
turns up the TV, buries his bunkered head
under tear gas pepper spray clouds,
under voices of the hundred thousand pandemic dead
and hundreds of thousands more to come,
buries his bunkered head
below the keening ghost-voice wail
from the millions murdered
down our four-hundred-year haunted tunnel of time—
hate-virus pandemic in all its mutated variants
burrowed into every fold of this rolling, pitted, puckered land,
bricked into every alley of our cities,
spike driven into every cell of our body politic—
ghost-voice wail of those enslaved
at our true founding
twined around every loop and whorl
of quill-pen calligraphy in our 4 July declaration,

haunting our constitution's every clause and amendment—
voices reborn in spirit harmony to lift
the chants from the peaceful street
from the blasted square
in pandemic anthem:

    Say their names
    All their names
    All their secret names

    Black Lives Matter
    Matter
    Must matter—

and what do orange man
and his flock know
    of pandemic?

and what do yellow hair
and his flock   choose to know
    of systemic?

See

If I could just get
everyone else
to love me
first

he thought

Then
I can go back
to the old man
and say

See?

An LA Freeway Songbook

LA's Emerald Jewelry

It's never more clear than after weeks of rain that LA's a city thrown down
Into the bowls made by mountains. As I drive the freeways that thread the hills
My eyes thrill to the emerald green that rises behind buildings and presses
the clouds.

Jam-Up on the Cat-Oh-Five

We live in the city of traffic jams on the 405 and other freeways.
This morning we had three cats bunched up on the patio outside our cat door
Competing for a lane. Elise's traffic report: "It's a jam-up on the cat-oh-five!"

Rearview Mirror Tableau, 5 Freeway South

She's passenger. He's driving.
Her face is angry and she speaks quickly.
She leans away from him. He leans toward her.

Homunculus Highway Brain Burrito

This 110 freeway with its tight lane miles I've driven so often, its gentle arc pass
into downtown
Through high-cut banks and herky-jerky flow, must surely be wrapped in a myelin
tortilla
In my brain—a well-traveled, intra-skull, neuronal network homunculus highway.

Rough Beauty

Hills driving north from LA on the 5 freeway display a rough beauty:
Mustard yellow, splotched with tufts of scraggly live oaks,
Hunched against drifty white clouds, skinned shoulders rust-veined.

On the Braided River

Up this ramp I join the braided river, its woven flow, currents and snags. Off right
freeway bank
Mountains rise snow-robed. Ahead, deep pink in great daubs across a lowering
blue horizon.
Souls by the millions for miles upon miles by wordless agreements we carve
this channel.

Years Within Years (Nahuatl New Year, El Sereno)

One Saturday in spring
in search of sandwiches
Elise and I chance upon
a café parking lot marketplace
in celebration of Nahuatl New Year
an ancient holiday
wholly new to us.

We walk among tables, racks, display cases
of handmade jewelry, masks, healing balms.
Wait for hot cacao-and-corn drinks in a raucous line
that spills out children from both ends and every side
all to raise funds for an Aztec culture charter school.

Here in Los Angeles, city I love made glorious
by all the peoples in this slow-turning world
come here on plumes of migration
stretched across centuries
there must be so many new years celebrated:
January 1st, Lunar New Year, Persian New Year,
Nahuatl New Year, Rosh Hashanah—
and how many others?

These years within years like crazy gears
interlocked on teeth of days
tumble us through each rolling twelve months—
Years within years within years.

In the Aztec marketplace
we see men with long braids, feathers in hat bands,
women in silver-and-stone jewelry.
Evident pride. A community
of the unconquered.

Sweet Elise Answers (Heart Tectonics)

At my center
this molten core of crazy questions
over slow pressure of years
has shifted my crusted creaking plates
and sometimes quakes my quiet mantle
or crashes my earth in fierce eruptions
that menace my innocent towns and villages.

But in my meeting and fusing with you
half a sweet crazed dozen
of all the most pressing questions
my life could ever pose were answered at once.
My center cooled, my surface slowed
and all my town and village doorways
filled with silent listeners

craning forward to hear the leaves
brushing green paintings on the sky.

In the Domed Chamber of Bone

Within and below the echoes
I peer up through
slanted sun-striped shadows

under the arching dome of bone
innermost secret chamber
of my skull

try to decipher the scratchings
berry paintings
oracular figures and letters

of strange and ancient origin.

Only Weeks From Death But With Life Still Possible

Peggy Holman 6/21/1940 - 4/18/2006

"I was out walking Dodger this morning and looking at the flowers,"
My mom said. "And I thought, I'm not afraid of dying.
But I love being alive."

Mission of San Juan Capistrano Ruins

People heaved these rocks up for walls
before they tumbled down.
People lie under the grass in this cemetery.

People walked these cold stone floors
and in this courtyard they gathered
the sun into their skin.

Nice Shoes in Atwater Village

Morning

"We can't afford those shoes," I say.

"You force me into this role," says Elise,
"You've had the same shoes for years.
"You need new ones. I buy them and you complain."

Afternoon

I bump into Susan, strolling in Atwater.

"Nice shoes," she says.

Holy Water in Koreatown

Private in my car I watch
an anxious mother
white-knuckle her boy's hand
across rush hour Sixth Street,
look with care left and right
all down the rapid running
of our long dangerous world.

He doesn't even notice
how close they pass
to the jaws and teeth of my car,
how it crowds the intersection,
eager to jump,
how the engine growls,
rumbles in fearsome crouch,
ravenous tiger on taut leash.

He just laughs and skips the length
of the racing-striped crosswalk—
playing hopscotch on a playground blacktop,
swinging his mother's jump rope arm—

surprises
a worn smile
onto her face

and a sudden sprinkling
of holy water
onto mine.

An Unplanned Planetarial Detour

Sunday afternoon
we set out for a movie
but we're having more fun talking.

So we veer off course
and find ourselves winding a narrow, corkscrew
Griffith Park road jammed with family traffic.

Halfway up, we park at a dizzy tilt on the dirt shoulder,
find a sidewalk bench where we hold hands and kiss,
gaze at the deep-cut, narrow, tree-lined canyon.

We rise to brave the steep
half-mile trudge in late afternoon sun
up to the plateau and observatory.

Under dreamy stars
on planetarium dome
in cushy chairs we doze.

God Toss

1.
I believe in the holy trinity:
the reptile brain, the limbic system
and the neocortex.

2.
In my cosmology, God arises from mind
as a planet emerges from spirals of astral dust
as a snowflake condenses from phantom water
as life sparks from organic molecules
shot through with ultraviolet.

Imagination runs always, a life form,
amoeba eternally subdividing,
perpetual motion organic machine.
It doesn't switch off. It doesn't burn out.

Half-blind, the *Voyager* probe still staggers
farther than the dying of the solar wind.
We cast our imagination out past the limits of our senses:
What came before us? Where does this I go
when the container it rides in dies?

God is the toss of imagination over death's fence.

God is an inevitable sprouting from the way
human imagination gathers and links pictures,
strings firefly flashes of thought into patterns,
scrabbles for a foothold on that fence
to leap over into the unseen.

God is guesswork. Resonant nonsense.

God is a single cloud shredding over hours in the sun,
then gone save for its imprint
on the human eyes that looked and saw it skidding by,
its stamp in the blood pumping through other human hearts,

in the transient memories of other human brains,
themselves only heavy gray clouds
shredding over long decades into soil.

The God the brain created will die when the body dies.

3.
In my other cosmology, God
is a flock of fireflies flashing in the dark.
God is unborn. God is aborning.
As life on our planet connects to life
on other planets, we string the neurons
that will fire between galaxies.
We knit the self-awareness
of the universe that will become
its brain, will become
God.

4.
In my theology

all that lives   goes to die

                and all that dies

goes to feed   all that lives.

Mind Full Suite

Grip

Sometimes it's a struggle just to stay in the now.
I grip my coffee cup
for dear life.

Planning Mindfulness

There I was in the shower this morning, rinsing my face under hot water
    and planning
moments in the future
when I would live in the present.

First Lesson

The book: *The Miracle of Mindfulness.* The plan: read it at the park with the dogs.
But we get to the park: no book. Driving home, I find it flapping and tattered
in the middle of the street. Seems I left it on the roof of the car and then
    drove away.

Chin-on-Paws Meditation

Through eyes lidded but not closed in meditation
I see my dog Red in soft focus pace in front of me, until at last
he gives up, lays at my feet, rests chin on paws. Acceptance.

Sitting Through

Only breath like waves moving on sand and receding. Only that. But muscles
between shoulder blades seize rope tight and burn. Waves of failure roll me
    on the sand:
I will never, how can I, I cannot. I throw my head back and yell *Goddammit!*
    But I sit through.

Shedding Moss

I am a stone.
I roll uphill
shedding moss.

Present Moment Meditation

Book in hand in hot bath, birds sing close out bathroom window, plane drones
far away.
Fragrance of my wife still in my beard floats to my nostrils on the in-breath.
Present moment, wonderful moment.

Mark, Hank Aaron, and the Skinny Honky

April 1974

Most days I sat next to Mark in fifth grade at Willow Street.
Memory's a poor time traveler
but I reach back to see him then—
small, shy, light-skinned
short, neat afro
head down
drawing on his blue notebook cover:

Black is Beautiful *Black Power*
A Black raised fist
Afro Power *Shaft*

his words in heavy block letters and cartoony rounded letters
shaded on the bottoms and corners
so they lifted off the notebook cover
or burrowed into it

underlined with lightning bolts
surrounded by flaring starbursts.

When I took my seat on April 9
I saw him focused
on his art
and I followed his eyes down
to a brand-new set of drawings:

Hank Aaron *715*
A raised bat gripped in two Black hands

Cool! I said.
Show me how you do that.

April 8, 1974

Hank Aaron hits homer 715 and shatters Babe Ruth's 40-year record.
The crack of Hank's bat
resounds
around
Stadium
America.

Some leap to their feet
throw fists in the air
and cheer.
Some clench their butt cheeks
onto their seats
ball their hands into fists
and rage

as if something they owned
had been stolen from them.

April 1973

Skinny honky!
You skinny honky!

Lynette and Veronica
yelled and kicked me
backed me into a corner
where two brick walls met
Recess, fourth grade.

Hate's a time-traveler
down the stroke
of a white-fisted billy club
in Alabama
rebounded up the legs and feet
of two Black girls
on a Michigan playground.

Skinny honky!
You skinny honky!

I didn't fight back.
I just took it.

April 1974

I liked to draw too
secretly on the lined paper inside my notebook
fantastic creatures I made up:

Freaky Flyer
a big circle for a head
wings coming off both sides
with jagged fringy feathers

V-Shaped Voogen Doogen
a big V with stick legs
upside down triangle eyes in the top of the V
and a V-shaped mouth with vicious teeth

too shy to show them even to Mark
but I copied his wording style for the captions.

March 24, 1970

After King
my mom brought me to see
on a hard metal folding chair
in an echoing gymnasium
before a huge screen
black-and-white scenes of cops
snarling
white fists
rage containers
brought their billy clubs down
again and again
beat and beat
Black men in dark suits and white shirts
Black women in flowered dresses
and Black kids my age,
seven.

I knew who the villain was
                                        my skin.
I knew who the hero was
                                        my age.

73/74

After the divorce, Mom sold my childhood home
on Junedale Drive, Kalamazoo, surrounded
by woods and fields, moved us to Lansing
where I knew no one, middle of fourth grade
straight into a majority Black class and there I was
the tall, skinny, long-greasy-haired white kid
and Laron threatened to beat me up
while Lynette and Veronica actually did.

A rental house on Lansing Ave, the white street
parallel to Roosevelt Ave and Knollwood Ave, the Black streets
the neighborhood kids told me never to walk alone
even three blocks out to Fabiano's Market
on the main drag Willow Street
for candy, pop, and comic books.

John and Russell lived three houses down
with their widowed father who rocked his round trunk
on spindly legs, shirtless, like some kind of pink spider
yelled and slapped his kids with a hand missing fingers
mangled in a machine on the line at the Oldsmobile plant.

Valerie, Joel and Jeff lived two houses down
with their big-busted, cigarette and gravel-voiced mom
divorced from their truck-driver dad
and we all sang along in their narrow, dark-paneled living room
with the dark green shag carpet
to *Convoy* and *Behind Closed Doors* on the console stereo.

And each day my mom drove out of industrial working-class Lansing
into the gentile tree-lined streets of neighboring college town
East Lansing for graduate school at Michigan State.

April 1974

I see myself sitting next to Mark in class
reading *The Once and Future King*
my heroes out of English myth and fantasy
King Arthur and Merlin
Bilbo, Aragorn, and Gandalf
fighting dragons and orcs
Black Knights and Dark Lords
with swords, spells, and ballads.

Mark's heroes were John Shaft, a Black private eye
going up against the whole honky city power structure
cops, mobsters, and politicians
with a big gun, swagger
and a deep-voiced soul-funk theme song

And Hammerin' Hank, who kept his eye on the ball
through a whiteout blizzard of hate mail
and death threats to summit a number
they said no one could climb with just a bat
sunder an abstraction with solid wood.

By '74 I ignored John and Russell's rule and walked to Fabiano's alone.
Not that I wasn't scared, but I minded my business and I was fine.

July 1974

A few months after Hank hit homer 715
my mom, professor now, married another professor
and we moved into my stepdad's house
in East Lansing, three blocks from the beautiful
Michigan State campus, with new stepbrothers and new friends
and a park across the street.

So in the long run of my life Lansing was a stumble, trip, and fall—
just a purple bruise and scraped knee
that scabbed over and itched while it healed

then blended back into my white skin
and the chances that go with it.

January 23, 2021

Hank Aaron died and I keep thinking about Mark.
Did he draw himself wings and fly away?
Maybe I passed him once driving a Mercedes on the Hollywood Freeway
or maybe he drew roots that dug deep and spread wide
under Lansing's packed dirt and patchy grass.
Did he grow a towering afro or long distinguished dreads?
A fearful image haunts: his drawing hand mangled in a factory machine.
A terrible thought troubles: his gentle spirit shredded
by the structures made in my honky image
to keep those in his down and outside.

Maybe he loved Lansing as I never could and walks it now proud and beautiful.
I don't remember his last name or what his father did for a living
whether he had brothers or sisters or anything about his mom.
Never went over to his house and he never came to mine.
I sat next to him most days and talked to him sometimes
but I was eleven and he was ten and I never knew him that well.
I know he was always more than white liberal notions
of a downtrodden Black kid.

He was a child. So was I.
I tried to be his friend and I think that's what we were.
Now he's grown up or gone forever.
I'll never know.

This is for Mark in your fullness
wherever you are.

Death and My Father

Chet Rogers 10/20/1939 - 9/26/2020

My stepmother called, said my dad might not last 24 hours
so I caught the first plane out of LAX at 9:35 p.m.
He died about the time I got off in Newark to change planes
but I didn't know until I landed in Charleston at 10:55 a.m.
and texted her as I raced toward baggage claim.
Call me, she texted back—and then I knew.
He had stopped breathing at 6:10 a.m. but his heart beat until 6:15.
She told the hospice nurse to leave him
until I could make it there to say goodbye.

I walked in their front door at almost noon.
Hugged her, rocked her, still masked.
The door to his room was cracked, shadowed.
Lisa, his caretaker, told me how much she loved him
then broke and turned her back, sobbing into her hand.
I paused at his door in reverence.
I knew what I would see. I knew that he was dead.
I thought that I would kiss him, stroke his cheek.
But Lisa, behind me, warned me not to touch him
without the blue gloves in a box on his desk.
Rigor mortis had set in, she said. If I had even tiny cuts on my skin
I could get infection. Death could pass into me.

When I pushed open the door and saw him, I gasped.
So pale, head on the pillow, mouth wide open and black.
Knowing and seeing are not the same. He was so dead. So gone.
He was there and not there. Never to be there again.
I gathered myself. Walked to his side. Stood next to
the railing of the hospital bed they'd brought in
when he could no longer make it upstairs to the bedroom.
I felt I owed it to him to witness. Scrutinize.
I felt I owed it to myself to hold him in my vision and memorize him
because soon they would take my father away and I would never see him again
on this Earth. I would have only my memories and this.

He was so white. The skin hugged the bones of his face. His head was tipped back
into the pillow. Soft clean pajamas, dark blue and forest green plaid.
White sheet pulled up to his shoulders.
The knuckles of his hands folded under the sheet
made a knobby projection. I felt thin, hollow, awkward. I stepped to the desk,
found the box of gloves dispensed like Kleenex, pulled out two.
I wrestled my thumb in, index finger, middle, yanking and squinching
and smoothing first one blue glove, then the next.
I was shaking. It felt absurd, but I had to do it to get back to him.

I returned to his side. With blue fingers I brushed the thin hair back
from his high broad forehead. Stroked his cheek. The flesh still had give.
So white. In death he was all angles. Sharp cheekbones like triangles.
The arch of his nose. Nostrils flared wide. Mouth like a cavern
deep into the earth. For the first time I knew where ghosts come from.
I've never seen one. Don't really believe in them. But now I understood.
Most of the humans who ever lived came before doctors and hospitals.
Death visited them often. In person. And they lived with their dead.
Saw them, skin drained of blood, so pale. One step from translucence,
two steps from a haunting. Skin tight on skull and mouth wide open
as if about to speak. It took nothing to imagine that if a soul rose,
floated away, it would rise through that opening.

I stood, and I looked, and I fought with the words that rushed
into my mind to describe him. I held to my breath and pushed the words away.
Words could come later. I wanted to be there, be in the not-words, with him.
I who live in words wanted to simply live in being. Life was gone from him
but it was in me and I could hold him there, living and dead.
My one fear was dispelled—that seeing him dead
would replace my images of him alive. They were not the same.
This was death. Not my father. My father alive will always live in me.
My father dead will die when I die.

Fed the Dogs Tune

There comes a time
when the earth is cold
and the dogs have all been fed
when I am left without a rhyme
or music in my head.

II.
GHOSTS OF THE LIVING

The One You Can't See in the Dark

I was happy to have a Black friend, proud of it even.
I still remember Charlie. His oval face, dark skin,
beautiful smile, easy and open.
I knew he liked me and he knew I liked him
and we both knew we both knew
both those things.

I met him at Ponderosa Steakhouse, junior year.
We bussed tables, washed dishes, flipped steaks together.
Pondo, as we called it, on Grand River in East Lansing,
was a sort of United Nations of surrounding high schools.
Dave and I went to East Lansing High,
Kendra and Colleen went to Okemos, Karen went to Perry.
I don't remember where Charlie went.

We were mostly white. Maybe all white, except Charlie.
But Charlie was cool. Cool but not too cool.
He blended right in.

Weekends, often, someone in the group
would invite the rest out to some party
in their neighborhood or small town,
Lake Lansing, Bath, Mason, or Dansville.
We'd meet their friends and family, see their houses,
see where and how they lived.

So this one night, early summer, warm out,
I brought my suave friend Frank from ELHS
out to one of these parties to meet the Pondo crew.
A cul-de-sac. Cars lined the street on both sides.
We walked toward the beacon of the open garage door,
keg inside by the two-step concrete stoop,
voices and light and music spilling out, Foghat or Styx or Rush.
People in knots on the driveway or seen through open curtains
into the living room. The high babble of blended talk and laughter.
Heads bobbing to the throb of rock 'n' roll.

As we came up the driveway, we met a cluster
of Pondo friends. Charlie was right in there.
I was happy to see him. I felt cool, like the guy
who knew everybody. A bridge between nations.
This is Frank, from EL, I told them. *Frank, this is...*
whoever and whoever else and some other.

> Then I said, *That's Charlie.*
> *He's the one you can't see in the dark.*

There was that pause—of a thing before it drops.
Then everyone laughed. Charlie laughed. I laughed. Frank laughed.
Whoever and whoever else and some other laughed.
I looked Charlie in the eye as the laughter died down and he grinned
and I grinned at him and I felt we had an understanding.
I felt he knew I'd made that little joke to flashbang
any racial tension so it lit the night, burned away,
and was gone. Tickled the elephant in the room until it fled,
giggling and holding its sides.

> But whose racial tension, anyway?
> Whose tension?
> *Whose?*

This was 1980 in Haslett or Williamston
or Shaftsburg in Michigan, not Los Angeles in 2020.
Maybe Charlie and whoever and whoever else
and I and Frank and all of us really did take it that way.
Maybe Charlie and I really did share that understanding.
Could it be that Charlie's laughter was spontaneous and real?

> Or was it just a laugh of survival?

Could be he'd felt like a secure point in the circle
then I slammed him in the chest and thrust him outside
so he stood there alone in a white spotlight
ringed by white teeth all pointed at him.

Quicksand Mirror

Aren't we still friends?
asks Anal Randy.

Can't bear to tell him
we never really were.

He tries to be nice
but something in him
sour, hard, small

is mirror enough
to scare the shit out of me.

This Leaky Vessel, the Word

I drop it
into the bottomless well
of mute feeling
draw it up brimming, teetering
try to haul it back full,
back to another
a loved one
a stranger
any who will listen
who will drink.

In my family
we did not touch.
Talk was our sacrament.
So I have this thirst in my chest cavity
for that connection of the breath that howls through the water
of the word carried from the tongue to the ear
but so much spills out
from the holes between letters
seams and joints between syllables.

I try to carry an ocean in a ladle
spill rivers and storms on my way
only to lift these precious drops left
haloed in the vapors of all that I've lost

to lips parted
                parched
                          for communion.

New Friend in Los Angeles

Why am I telling you all this? she says.
I haven't even told my sister all this.

I don't know, he says, *but you do realize*
I'm gonna spread it all over town now, right?

She laughs
and touches the back of his hand.

She's telling him
how she first made love
to her new boyfriend in Colombia
and all the delicious craziness that came after.

He holds his chin in his hand, smiling.
I know exactly what you mean, he says.
I remember that feeling well.

Go on, he says, *so what happened*
after he struck his match that way
and turned you on?

He feels his smile waver
with wishing
she'd fall for him instead.

I think I'm gonna have another beer,
he says.

The waitress swoops in with cheesecake.
She digs in.

Y'know, he says
I think there's a touch of mourning
in any man-woman friendship.

She laughs
and nods vigorously between mouthfuls.

LA Area Precinct-Walk Impressions

Scottish Frijoles (Pico Rivera, Sunday Evening)

I walk the streets with Scottish names: Loch Alene, Eglise, Kilgarry,
but from nearly every door that opens to my knock the earthy rich fragrance of frijoles
burbling on kitchen stoves wafts out until it follows me from house to house.

A Notion of Ocean Pervades (Redondo Beach, Saturday Morning)

Salt-air weathered wooden houses with ship's deck porches and crow's nest balconies
yearn for the unseen sea. Wind-twisted old trees with leaves whipped like tattered sails.
Tank-topped women and shirtless men deep-tanned. Gulls cry from over the hills seaward.

Four Stoops (Pico Rivera, Election Night)

At my knock, a little girl's voice: *For my daddy?* Her brother: *Dad, some guy's at the door!*
Cockatiel in porch cage hops on perch as chihuahuas crash snarling against security door.
Bamboo wind chimes knock knuckles. Next stoop: faux-bamboo ceramic wind chimes clink.

A Toe's Radius

Tonight my sleep no longer lonely.
Alone can be sweet—
covers off
sliding glass door open to the overnight balcony
air blowing cool across my naked skin.

But all tonight long, even in sleep
I feel her warm body
under covers
so near—
within a toe's radius.

Give Me Questions

On the eve of Gulf War, August 1990

In countries
much east
tank treads
churn ocean of sand
to black froth.
The dictator, our mad bandit
mustachioed villain
hides in his palace
counting on his fingers
silently re-figuring, silently praying
while billion dollar birds mad to fall
on anything that moves in that desert
fill sky, running oil-black trails of bile.

Every liar, they say,
someway reveals his bluff:
the fugitive flick of the eyes
a small betrayal of the vocal timbre
some covert signal-truth of the body.
Tonight the president addresses
a fearful nation and I watch
for the tell.
Eyes unwavering
shoulders square
his pinched repertoire of gestures
coached and choreographed
it's clear he's been prepped
rehearsed to the point
of intended inscrutability.
Still, before long there it is.
Gradually, almost imperceptibly
our commander-in-chief
begins to lean ever so slightly
away from the camera
backward and to the right.

Over twenty minutes
he shifts less than an inch
but it's a clear move
toward escape, a backing out
and away, as some last nugget
of conscience in his cells
struggles to tug him back
from that biggest of lies:
The killing lie. The lie
of no return.

All across America
the armchair patriots
can only moan and whine
"Give me liberty
from fear of death!"
On soggy paper plates
that buckle
under such weight
of gray lard
they offer up their brains
to the govern-
mental spokespersons
who murmur
from deep within
TV news-cushions.

Give me questions to crack bedrock,
jackhammer foundations.
Questions to pound skulls
thick with paste and calcium,
pounding
from deep inside
with sharp beat
of heart truly fearful
for first time,

for first time wide-open
breathing.
Questions to unstop arteries
clogged up by years
of rancid sludge cynicism.
Give me questions thick as chemical porridge,
rust-colored questions.
Questions hard
as muscle strangled
in steroid-twisted
wire veins, give me questions.
All I ask is questions.

Rio de Los Angeles After the Storm

A day after the storms of a week
I walk the path at the river park.
Cumulus clouds with purple underbellies
shade the hills and ring my horizon
tumble upward in white billows
into a sky crowning baby blue above them.

I face this pure vista
and the words to describe it
barrel in to lay claim, jostle,
elbow their way into my mind.

I want to reach upward into that blue
swipe the words away, drive
one fierce breath into them,
part them side to side and
skid them across the horizon—

The clouds can stay.
It's only the words
that trouble my view.

It Goes On It Goes

Matthew Butcher 1983-2010

Today I am sad for my friend and her family.
Her son shot, killed. And grief is because time
only goes one way, so we laugh and joke,
drink and smoke, eat and hug and say
soft words close that help but only
so much and briefly because time
only goes one way, it goes on it goes

Elegy to the Mystic Poet Died Young

for Tony Clay

I would say to you
You can be wild and still.

I would say to you
You can learn to make your magic
without dragging around that sackful
of tools and toys.

I would say to you
You can learn to take up the rhythm
of the rolling bellows breath in your chest
for your rhythm, the music
of the soft hiss of the blood in your veins
for your music, rather
than being danced and pulled
by all that crazy howling around your ears.

I would say to you
You can become enchanted instead
by the altered state
of throwing echoes
down the bottomless well
of your own need.
You can become entranced instead
by the altered state
of falling back
into the open arms of space.
You can become enthralled instead
by the altered state
of coming up slowly
through the afterimage
of your own dream.
You must become addicted instead
to the altered state
of crouching in quiet at glade's edge
and watching your own thoughts
like wild animals in the field.

And I would say to you
With the help of luck
and trust, you may find
that the true voice
is the one that will not shout to be heard
over all that frenzied motion
is the one that will not chase you down
through all that frantic running-after-seeking
is the one that can be heard as clearly
as you may see the paths and lines
in your own hand at rest on your own knee
when you learn
to be wild and still.

Balloon Haiku

To be written on balloons

Sly whispers exchanged
over the heads of children
balloon to balloon

Sky looks down on blue
balloon, fluffs its thin white hair
in its reflection

Wish I were see-through
like this balloon, so you could
spy my hidden heart

Oh if you would just
kiss me with that so-sweet mouth
I would surely die

Only you, dear one
hold the intimate power
to so deflate me

Lone balloon longed to
evolve by folding into
balloon animal

Balloon's recurring
dream was an ever-shrinking
and empty nightmare

My inflatable
heart is stuffed so full of love,
why, I could just pop

Just a ghost in a
wet suit, I love to go out
diving in the sky

In my arms our dog
Red passed with a gentle sigh
like a child's balloon

Free Will on the Off Chance

So what is chance?
Each moment the universe blinks
and wakes all over again.

Then what is free will?
Each moment the universe blinks
and wakes all over again.

Blinks and wakes all over again.

Coffee

by Scott Roat and Jeff Rogers

Black and silver spools,
an uncoiling ribbon,
architecture of feverish reveries
built on bricks of beans;
an egg, blue, sliding across the plate,
a slick track of oil collects at the lip;
wash it away with coffee, holy coffee,
energy oil, tincture of high wire nerves;
the sleepy reason, as clouds part,
releasing Gothic sunshine curves
as the first drop uncoils
from the black spool, warming my mouth;
illusion of time returns uncoiling
in a black and silver morning stretch;
the crisp skin of bacon overcooked
crumbles its brittle bones between my teeth;
membrane of egg peeled back from plate,
slivers of crunch potato, tears of crunch bread;
thin dollops of purple jam crease the corners
of my mouth; all to bed the stream
for black and silver baptism, all for steam
and rush of holy bean distilled: a gemstone,
a black diamond in the center of the plate,
unconscionably large, black, and unashamed,
sacred tincture between earth and sky,
ageless compression of the holy bean;
balm for the weary, prop for the weak,
mediator for disputes of philosophers,
centerpiece at the peace table,
shameless bean carry me off to breakfast,
where I swell with the day—release, release!
Lay me back in gentle brown river uncoiled.

Airport Poem (Halfway There)

I need you to see for yourself, my stepmother said.
My dad's dizziness, the falling down, the walker at home
and the cane for the evening walks from the handicapped space
to each night's Italian restaurant or Irish pub
or dockside bar and grill, on a regular rotation
that follows their favorite bartenders,
the ones who give the most generous pours.
Two chardonnays at lunch every day, two scotches at dinner,
three or four tall glasses full of ice and Johnny Walker
each night at home before he falls asleep in his chair.
She bought me a roundtrip ticket.

So for me, for now, it's the stool in the airport bar,
limbo's sweet station
for this next one peaceful hour
with nowhere else I have to be,
an hour that will disappear down a hole in time
never after to be accounted for,
with its throat-stab of straight whiskey
paired with the cold bite of pale ale
for which there can be no known consequence,
the alcohol eased well out of my system
long before I arrive anywhere
where anything I say to anyone
will matter after it's said.

Nothing to worry about, I tell myself
in this lovely, delicious purgatory
between home, already behind me
and John's Island, South Carolina,
in that shimmering future into which I can push
the true and rehearsed mission of my quest:
the talk with my dad that I fear to have
but know I must. Have known for years that I must.

And here in limbo I have this trusty paperback
in my back pocket, talisman ready to hand

with its sleek silver spaceship on the cover,
a crew of courageous rebels aboard
ready to risk it all.
In the magic of these next few lost hours,
may their courage come into me
through some alchemy of fictional transference.

My dad and I have always loved to drink together
and settle down to business—tell the old stories,
hold forth, get thick-voiced and teary-eyed
because our ancient English blood must be diluted with spirits
before the emotions can flow.
And so the irony will not be lost on either of us
that I'll have to get drunk with him myself
up way past his wife gone discretely to bed
to tell him I believe his drinking is killing him,
even knowing damn well all the while
that it won't make a goddam bit of difference.

Communal Best

Walking around Silver Lake Reservoir
the norm seems to be
little to no eye contact
so I'm free to watch
all the faces go by.

A young Latina, chatting on her cellphone,
pushes a white baby in a stroller.
Pairs of jaunty white women gab and gesture. They part
to pass me, cleave together with no break in pace of step or talk.
Runners and fast walkers, young old and middle,
groove in public solitude to their personal earphone soundtracks.

A sleek young Black woman with tight braids,
eyes straight ahead, kicks her knees high as she flies on by.
An older white man in droopy-brimmed gray hat
nods in rhythm with his stride, brim bouncing
as he plods on, face determined, watching his feet
and the path before him, pushing through.

In calligraphy on brows and cheeks I read
joy, doubt, and worry, I see
the setting of resolve,
I see

Everyone's just trying
to do their best.

Baby Naked Song

And so I long to recall the secret
        of standing in space without falling
And so I long to recall the secret
        of flaring into wild happiness without flying apart
And so I long to recall the secret
        of new raw skin unstung

And so I long to recall the peace
        of hatching in a nest of silence
And so I long to recall the power
        of watching through clean water
And so I long to recall the reflex joyous pride
        of standing baby-naked to air and human seeing

And so I—
            unbeliever—
                        long to recall

Mother God's soothing
                        lilting words
                                    of nonsense

Carry Me Off to Breakfast

Born to be a salad,
Heavy on the dressing.
Write a greenish ballad,
Oh what a purple blessing!

Trained to be an egg white
All lumpy, fat, and free.
When scrambled in the Teflon,
How happy we would be!

Stoned into a meathead,
Pink along the inside,
Fried atop the coalbed,
Black is on the flipside.

Groomed as for a lady,
Thin and tall and flighty,
White and never fadey,
A-goin' to be a bridey.

Wrapped up in the tinfoil,
Stowed refrigerator.
Spoil is not the gargoyle.
Scrape it 'cross the grater.

Paul's an English muffin,
Art's a soggy cornflake,
John's a dried-out lemon,
Put 'em in a pancake!

Born into a cornfield,
Raised to be a wheatfield,
Drafted for the Ziegfeld,
Pushed it through a spyglass.

Fed with Daddy's pigsty,
Gave 'em lots of candy,

Brushed it with an eyeglass,
Mailed it out and dandy.

Met her at the bus stop,
Danced her through a turnstile,
Dressed her for the party,
Gifted with a new smile.

Carry me off to breakfast,
Spill it on the bedspread,
Spell it on the freezer:
"A limit to the bloodshed."

Blogger Old Potatoes

The minibulbous gravy trickled down her chin.
Soft, warm and slagey, it made the girl grin.
Plopped down on potatoes, it made potatoes drown.
Good girl to eat those, she wolfed the buggers down.

Blogger old potatoes! She threw them on the wall—
Decorate the kitchen, decorate the hall.
Decorate the doggy, hear the doggy speak.
Decorate her Mommy, hear her Mommy shriek.

The little girl she giggles, cackles at the chaos,
spiggles at the wimpole, frowns at dental floss
between old Mommy's fingers, when girl is put to bed.
On stubborn bits Mom lingers, and gently holds her head.

Blogger old potatoes! Stuck between her teeth.
Stuck between her big toes (decorate her feet).
Squish them in the sheets now, Mommy never knows
'til Mommy checks the hamper where the laundry goes.

In wishful little dreams now, on squishy rugs she flies:
rugs of mashed potatoes, while rapid move her eyes.
Her sticky feet in slumber kick within the bed,
while gently grows the little smile that decorates her head.

Connective Tissue

Life an endless conference
of cloud ideas
with earth facts
with street curb facts.

We live in the sky—
connective tissue
muscle
between heaven and earth,
deeps of mind and deeps of touch—
flexed and released
in turn
by each.

We are sinews, ligaments—
heaven depends on us,
earth depends on us,
not to cut loose
from either.

Lovemaking—
the perfect marriage
of these clouds and this earth,
this heaven and this
turf-wrapped stone,
clod of organic
and lifeless,
soluble and solid.

Tree rooted in strata
plunges
into wide-open sky
hands upward leaves
and frost into heaven.

The Softness and the Melting Fire

Lover's Map

She the round Earth
and I the continents
wrapping my arms around her.

Choose Your Moment

Her lips soft, exploratory. An invitation. But I need to look for jobs.
Is that wrong? I ask. *Should I just be in the moment?*
Depends what moment you want to be in, she says.

Making Love in the Blood of Her Moon

She's cramping so I massage her belly but oh my hand strays lower.
Making love she brings finger to mouth, leaves a red crescent.
Drawn out my shaft is bright, my base is dark with glory red.

My Orgasm, Gently

Pulled out of me
as on a long thin silken strand
blooming wide a blanket of clouds filled up with light.

Two Fingers

It's like she's climbing them.
She pushes slowly down, arches, moans amazement.
Two fingers inside for a long time as we smile, kiss, and talk.

She Calls It Comfy Bedness

Chilly cave under blankets, waking sweet naked and gathering in.
Warm skin all along warm skin, together stretching legs, toes.
Bright smile close, fumbling sleepy kisses, hands smoothing hair.

The Answer

I awake in the dark to her palm drawing questions on my chest
and I am the answer.
I am the answer to her hand.

The Softness and the Melting Fire

My wife looked so beautiful at dinner and when I park at home
in the dark as if on first date I kiss her with senses tuned high—
exquisite the softness and the melting fire.

Time Blossoms

Jasmine vine
over days unwatched,
stretched and thinned,
dangled upward,
curled itself around black iron
canopy uprights
in a green scrollwork so delicate
it glows from the inside,
a vein coursing sunlight.

Its first white starflowers, tiny-rayed,
open, exhale their first
faint sweet breaths.

The months since planting
by turns patient and anxious
have now flowered
in these blossoms of time
hanging off
the retreating year.

Ghosts of the Living

I fear no nighttime visits from my dead.
I've hoisted my own mother's casket—as light as her gentle spirit flown.
No, it's only the ghosts of the living who haunt my waking dreams.

Anyone who's lived as long as I has lost those gone to grave or ash,
So I'm followed now by a spectral entourage, lively, fond, and sad,
And I fear no nighttime visits from my beloved dead.

It's the words unsaid and deeds unjustly done
To loved ones still alive that nail me sleepless to my bed,
These ghosts of the living who haunt my waking dreams.

They'll pop up grinning with a headlight sweep in my midnight rearview mirror
Or stalk me at noon the lonely length of a harsh-lit office hallway.
No, I fear no nighttime visits from my dead.

It's the sudden name long undialed that troubles my cell phone fingers,
Wails to me in the faucet stream as I wash my morning dishes—
These ghosts of the living who haunt my waking dreams.

Things I've done to the woman beside me kick me awake in our bed,
Rap their skeleton knuckles on the mad attic doors of my mind.
No, I fear no nighttime visits from my beloved dead.
It's these restless ghosts of the living who haunt my waking dreams.

In Spaceships

they ask ya four times
to pass the salt

and on the fifth time
you get *pissed off*

and you scramble up
spill it
try to corral it in your fingers
wave your arms at it

as it floats
out of those little holes in the shaker

and sprinkles the atmosphere…

Right Wrong Night Song

I've done you wrong
          I've done you right.
You're still the one I reach for
          In the center of the night.

I've done you right
          I've done you wrong
You're still the one I sing to
          When I improvise my song.

III.

EVERYTHING ALIVE MOVING

The White Liberal Poet Organizes a Reading Against Racism

I'm not ashamed to say it, but I cried like a baby through John Lewis's funeral.
And I must have watched the BLM protests 24 hours a day for a solid week.
Would have been out there myself except for my co-morbidities—
can't risk the COVID.
But I fucking hate racism.
That's why I left my hometown and moved to Los Angeles—all those
damn racists I grew up with. We don't have that problem
on the LA poetry scene, thank God.

And that's why this idea just possessed me—
that I had to pull together a whole bunch of my favorite
powerhouse poets for a big reading against racism.
Man, we're gonna get in some good trouble.
We're gonna make a statement.

We've got a great lineup already. Everyone wants to do it.
I've got feelers out to three Black poets and one Latino
and I sure hope one of them gets back to me before that last slot gets filled.
'Cause we've got Kenneth Bishop, the old neo-beat Buddhist communist
bebop jazz poet. He's going to do fifteen minutes from his 100-page epic
Horseshit Highway Manifesto, where he roadtrips across racist America
from coast to coast tripping balls on acid shrooms pot and peyote.
He savages the South, bulldozes the Midwest,
and puts a stake through the heart of the plains states.
Everywhere but here, he chants, *Everyone but me.*
He's got a lotta rhythm for a white dude—LOL.
Man, we're gonna make a real statement.

Jennifer Pepper, that hot young blonde poet, is gonna do her poem
called "Swipe Left Bitch, You Know I Don't Fuck Racists."
And look. You gotta check out her Instagram. Scroll down
to those bikini photos where she shows off all her tats.
Just got word that Nick Bundt wants to be on the bill.
You remember him—from his old punk band Waxing Gibbous,
when he went by the name Giggy Ballsack?

He's got this piece called "I Pronounce Myself Guilty"
where he confesses every racist thought he's ever had.
It climaxes with him screaming *Forgive Me! Love Me!*
while he yanks out clumps of his own hair
and flings them at the audience. Then he
breaks down sobbing and pounding on the floor.
He makes a gorgeous catastrophe of his own feelings.
We're gonna make a righteous statement with this thing.

I sure do hope one of those Black poets gets back to me soon
before someone else nabs that last spot
because this is a real important fight, taking down racism.
Gloria Glitter, the 80s party-girl poet, is doing her signature piece
"Color is Just a Trick of the Light." It's kind of her
"Stairway to Heaven." Starts out as a lyrical ode
to sex, drugs, and her Black lover who was shot by the cops
and then builds to a soaring crescendo on how race
has no scientific validity and we're all just children of Africa
and if we'd only realize it we could all live as one family.
See what I'm sayin? A statement, man, we're making a fuckin' statement.

I really thought about getting Mike the Poet to do his
hip-hop LA history stuff, but he always insists on
bringing along a whole flock of his urban high school students.
And I mean, they're talented and all, and it's downright noble,
but I'm not sure they're right for this crowd and
we don't really have time for all that. We gotta
keep the program moving. So instead I've got
Jerry Reynolds, that kinda intellectual-looking poet with
the longish gray hair, beard and glasses.
Looks a little like Steven Spielberg?
He does these real ironic, Joycean, Lewis Carroll wordplay-type poems
and he's got this one called "Life on Singing Street" which is just
a devastating takedown of 70s white flight suburbia.

Still no response from those Black poets, though.
Such a great opportunity for them, I can't figure it out.
Frankly, at this point, I almost hope they don't get back to me.
Sometimes it's just easier to go with the poets you can relate to.

If I'm being real honest—just between you and me—
I'm kinda scared of those Black poets. I always feel like
they're judging me. I'm always sure I'm gonna say something wrong.
Seems like every damn day there's five more ways to fuck it up.
And who wants to feel that guilty all the damn time, anyway?
I mean, *goddammit*—
it shouldn't be this hard,
should it?
We've got a statement to make
against racism.

Mom Laughs

When I was a kid, my mom
would sometimes laugh at me.
I'm sorry, she'd say
when she saw my face.
I think I knew she wasn't trying to be mean.
It still made me feel weird.

Once I told her
if she didn't give me what I wanted
I'd never speak to her again.
She laughed a merry laugh
that just rolled right out
like a stream over stones in sunlight.
It hurt. I felt confused.

That would make me very sad
she said, and I immediately relented.

Ten years ago my mom was dying of pancreatic cancer.
It's hard to be a human, she often said with a vocal shrug.
We had some great conversations those last four months.
I can still picture driving Sixth Street east to work
through the tunnel of lavender jacarandas
as we speculated on whether some part of us lives on
and she talked about her own mother after death.

Her refrigerator was always meticulous, my mom said.
Everything neatly packed and hand-labeled with a throwaway date.
Sometimes when I'm digging through the smelly fridge
for whatever spoiled, I can feel her laughing at me.
Over the cellphone Mom hears my confused silence.
Not in a mean way, she says.

My wife and I don't have kids.
We have two dogs, four cats, and a bird.
This morning, I laughed at our dog Chewie.
Chewie knows that cats eat first, then dogs.
But he was standing inches from rickety old cat Vinnie
while she finished her breakfast.

Chewie, out! I said. He skulked away,
sat down, hurt look on his face.
I welled up with love and laughed at him.
I couldn't help it. He looked confused.
Sweet boy, I said, and ruffled
the scruff behind his ears.

My mom is ten years dead. A long time for me.
For her, it's just the beginning.
A few months after she died I bought a book
I thought she'd like and only then remembered
it was her birthday.
But I didn't feel her laughing at me.
Sometimes I wish she would.

Until this morning, when I laughed at Chewie.
Not in a mean way. A laugh of love.
My mom laughed with me.
And all at once I understood.
I could have almost run my hand down
through my own eight-year-old self's hair
and said, *Sweet boy.*
You miss your mom, don't you?

COVID Killer Blues

First comes the fever like flames behind my eyes
The fever comes first blazing behind my eyes
Burning up inside till I thought that I would die

Chills come next like ice inside my bones
Next come the chills like ice inside my bones
Got my wife too, so at least I'm not alone

Happy to be alive
Happy to be alive
Thought I was a goner
But I wouldn't take the dive

Sheer exhaustion come, dropped me on the bed
Pure exhaustion come, pinned me to the bed
I felt just like a zombie, the barely living dead

COVID crawled inside me, shat inside my lungs
Crawled right down inside me, infiltrated my lungs
Now I'm so goddam grateful every time I see the sun

Grateful to be alive
Grateful to be alive
I tell you sir and madam
I'm grateful to be alive

The virus whispered, *Hey, you know I'm gonna slay you*
That virus whispered, *Son, I'm gonna up and kill you*
But don't worry none, I'm gonna kill your wife too.

You son of a bitch, I said, *I'm not gonna let you take me*
Son of a bitch, I said, *be damned if I let you kill me*
When I wake up to see the sunrise you know it's gonna thrill me

Happy to be alive
Happy to be alive
What doesn't kill you makes you long haul
Still I'm happy to be alive

It's a long hard road back up the hill to health
A long rough climb back up the hill to health
How it adds up now, only need my life for wealth

I'm happy to be alive
So happy that we're alive
Well, we're most of the way back—
We'll drop a postcard when we arrive

Several hundred thousands weren't as lucky as me
We mourn for all the thousands not as lucky as we
Those loved ones who we miss, who we'll never again see

We're grateful to be alive
Happy to be alive
Now sing it sister brother
We're happy to be alive

Fever Dream Lullaby Broken

1.
Smear of red and blue lizard guts
in the white porcelain bathtub this morning,
cat Pepper's favorite arena for the kill.
Last night 3 a.m. raccoons erupted
in screech and chatter, drove our little dogs
half wild. They snarled and leaped off the bed
shoved through the dog door, barked
and pawed the loose dirt to scrabble up the hill.
I stalked naked into the dark yard to pull them back.

Hot nights lately, the Santa Ana winds
drum the windows, rip fronds from the palms,
rattle the sliding glass doors in their tracks.
One kick of the earth in her twitchy sleep
could pitch this whole house
off the hill into the street.

2.
This morning at the river park
signs warned of coyote sightings.
Drought drives them hungry from the hills.
But we let the dogs off leash and terrier Franklin
pranced down the embankment into the trees.

I heard his death-fear yelp. Terror visions
of my little dog torn to bloody meat jumped my mind
as I plunged into the brush where I saw the coyote
astride him, brindled brown and big as a German shepherd.
I yelled Franklin's name and the dog ripped free,
one long fang gash in the powder-blue t-shirt
that protects his allergic skin.

Coyote just stood there
millions of hard years in his eyes.
You are the interloper, they seemed to say.
I charged him and roared
waved my long arms.
He just turned and loped away.

3.
Crosstown later
I parked my car at a meter.
A crow stood in the street
pecked at a dead squirrel in a splash of red
soaking pink into the pavement.
Through one black globe eye
he looked at me
as if to say
You are the stranger here
unfit for this landscape.

The sky reared up, shoved
against the ghost-blue membrane
that held back the teeming asteroids and unseen stars.
The broken-toothed skyline ducked against the blow.
Beneath my feet, Earth's thin turf skin
seething with life, rumbled
like the lid that clatters atop a boiling pot.

Crow bobbed his head
dipped his spear-point beak
ground sharp on the wheel
of geologic time, and tore
at the carrion flesh
of my pending extinction.

Milk Jar Ditty

I move through the days
like milk
                    over the lip
of a jar.

One day
                    I'll sour up
and curdle away.

End Sea Begin Sky

We hike the moonlit crooked path on down.
Bear of a forest hulks behind our backs.
The lights of San Francisco tilt in stacks
That perch atop the ocean like a crown.
The crescent San Francisco curves aloft
Stretches into the middle of the sky
Weaves into the when of where and why
Blends into the sharp of dark and soft.
Can't tell where splash of splayed out urban lights
Quite bleeds into the spray of stars like dust
Or feeds into the vision-craving lust
This laughing psychedelic starry night.
If this is what it always was to be
Then it will ever be enough for me.

All Asleep and All Good

My wife Elise
lies on the couch
propped on pillows
TV for a lullaby
cheek cradled in palm
lower lip drooping

and she is again a sweet little girl
pretty child
all asleep and all good.

Freeing the Balloons

On the edge of Beverly Hills, 1984

At the House of the Oh-So-Lonely-Hamburger
in the hot stuffed confines of a bricked-in booth
clown-windowed to the sun
on this private birthday
in this public restaurant
in some sky-blue July or so
I pushed back the window, elbowed
the cash register and microphone aside,
and carried across three strings between my fingers
leading three bobbing balloons
knocking together and all about the upper regions
of the brown-bricked outside, yellow-tiled inside booth
before they
                    POPPED
                                        out of the window
and released from the hand of the gentle outlaw
danced away up to a cloud, crowded
bumping there under it for a moment,
and then off again
into a smog-rimmed bright-blue dream
of knighthood for the freeing of balloons.

Bleak LA

Queen of the Street (Piss on You All)

Walking down 7th to Langer's, looking down at iPhone, I see a naked butt crack.
Woman squatting on sidewalk, hiss, and urine hits concrete, trails toward gutter.
As I pass, she stands, yanks up ratty black underpants with defiant authority.

No Faith

Driving down Vermont, I see a man lying on pavement next to bus bench, boots off curb.
White beard, red face, hand in pocket—no, down pants front, stroking, but idly.
No rhythm, no faith. Untouchable, he is alone in public view and always will be.

Pasadena Movie Theater Men's Room Waystation

Funny the instant messages intuition delivers. As I enter he shies away, and
even before I smell him, or see his three backpacks, or see him washing in sink
and drying with paper towels, I know that he's homeless. Eyes to myself I step to urinal.

The Lennon Killer

I'm sporting my new '75 Lennon cut when he stamps my way, wild gray hair in flight around
sunburned face, yells, "Mark David Chapman!" Lennon's last words *I'm shot* ricochet
in my skull. "He thought he was *justified!* But God won't forgive him on judgment day."

Bum Ritual

Each time I see him, settled on sidewalk, exchange always goes the same:
"Can I bum a cigarette?" In his grizzled old folksy timber. "Sorry. Don't smoke."
"Don't start any bad habits. I got enough for both of us."

Quandary of the Beloved

He's so in love with me!
she tells her girlfriend
in smiling wonder
at the table next to mine.

She hunches forward
and drops her voice:
Should I be worried?

Walked Up From Sunset

I sit at the bus stop. “Hey man!”
Shit, somebody wants something.

Homeless, begging for money.
Maybe lost, needing directions.

I look up. “Here, I walked up from Sunset.”
He hands me an unused transfer.

Car Stereo Jukebox

Listening to Led Zeppelin in the Car

Page's guitar with hummingbird speed and delicacy, raven-bodied thickness.
Bonham's drums with nimble heavy tread dancing on the rocks in the wildflowers.
Plant's macho falsetto, fourth and equal instrument in the band—stringed wind,
to be exact.

Listening to Neil Young in the Car

In such command of the colors of his instrument—
His electric broad, heavy, and deep. Acoustic strung with sunlit sand.
His voice shot through with light, thin reed floating on water.

Silence Shared

Sitting on the floor in the dark
we just stop talking.
I become aware
of a thorough silence.
I become aware of her
awareness of the silence.

I open up my pores to the silence.
She guards the silence for me
and I for her. Our breathing
pushes slowly in and out
of the silence. I notice
silence in the corners of the room,
and sounds outside, behind us:
traffic far away, voices
from the apartment building next door.
I hear a car idling in the parking lot
and smell the gas drifting in at the window.
I feel my palm resting on my thigh,
feel the weight and cushion
of flesh resting on coarse denim.

I notice how my right ankle meets
the hardwood floor, neither budging,
until my ankle begins to feel
like a knot in the wood.
It occurs to me to stroke her shoulder
with my hand draped around it
but this would be wrong
would be like a small boy jumping
up and down yelling for attention,
would break faith with the silence.

After some while someone speaks.
Doesn't matter who, or what's said.
The silence simply fills and flows over
like the moment a bathtub overflows.
You can see the water rise
just above the lip of the tub
and stay there, then with grand slowness
push over the edge and down
in a sheer curtain. The silence
ends that way, natural force
pushing it out of its path
and changing it
into something else.

Later,
when kisses and murmurs
of goodbye come, she says
Thank you for the silence.

Time Sings the Universe

Time
is the path we take
through the universe,
anything but straight.
Our path is made
of what we notice.

Probability wave
swirls,
snaps into
particulate place—
when we see it
where we catch it
when we look.

All moments in time
exist now
in dimension.
Observation
fixes outcome.

Probability waves
and elementary particles.
Eleven dimensions
of superstrings.
Dark matter.

What we observe
becomes.
What we fail to see
remains unfulfilled.
A weighty charge.

So artists
who make form from chaos
are world-builders.
Master meditators
with indiscriminate
unwavering attention
are as gods.

In fact,
incipient god
looks out through your eyes
on the shapeless nebula
of cosmic jelly,
and everywhere
sees and so makes
form and substance.

Time
is the tale,
the tally,
of what we have yet seen
out of all else that will
one day be seen.

We are the way
the universe learns itself.
We are the way
the universe resolves itself.
We are the song
the universe sings itself.

Time is the ruler
made of periodic pencil scratchings
on the doorjamb that measures
the growth of god.

God first wakes
at the end of time.
God dies
at the beginning of time.

God is the self-awareness
of the universe.

Time has
no end
and no beginning.

This Body Me

Not alone these thoughts
housed in this tower
lost above the cloudline

I am also this body
rooted where the stone column's feet
kick through the sod and enter the dirt.

Told this morning
by my stepmom
how my dad battled bedsores
for three days this week
no longer able to stand on his own
no longer able to walk—
dizzy, balance lost
incontinent
diapered at night
leaking into the sheets
unable to clean himself
his eighty-year-tall tower felled
toppled onto the field of his bed.

All day long
my professor father
eloquent and articulate lifelong
the walls of his tower profuse
with proofs of his accomplishments
diplomas and proclamations
yelled out
My ass hurts!

Locked in my own fifty-seven-year-tall tower
its architecture so much the same as his
I ponder how much I even know
this structure that holds me above the clouds.

I can almost feel it stagger
sway
clutch at the air
at the very thought
and I feel dizzy, sick.
I could throw up.

How much of what brought him down
was built into the very stones?
Our stones?
How much was neglect,
abuse, subtle sabotage?
If I learn this body
me
better now
can I still shore up my tower,
choose a different fate?

Boxed in by teetering stacks of books
piles of papers
in this tower of words
I get messages from below.

Sometimes I hear steps on the stairs
a pounding on the heavy chamber door.
Not now! I yell back.
Just let me finish this stanza!

I hear rustling
a note slipped under.
I snatch it up, glance at it
toss it into a drawer
with all the others:

Your left knee has been hurting for three days,
it might say, or
You can't ignore that hitch in your chest
when you take a deep breath.
Even:
You've been drinking every night lately.
Time to cut back.

Now I look out from my tower
at billowy tops of clouds
lit by rays of sun
and resolve
to climb down
all those stone stairs
into the depths of this body, me,
and count them as I descend,
to survey what lies below.

Verses of Earth Refrain

Crunch
as I tear the chest cavity
of the chicken carcass in two
to feed my dogs.
                    Sheen of grease
coats my fingers, life juices of the bird
who once breathed, squawked, flapped wings
or slammed them against hard bars
of a too-small cage, packed in with too many
other birds.
              I dig at the webbing of meat
between tiny bones of the wings,
scrape out pink white brown stuff
between the ribs, gouge
little black spongy organs, strip
the smooth pink breast muscle.

So that no chunk of this being
built up and slaughtered for us
will go unused.
So this phoenix descended
will transform and then rise.

Wings and ribs, meat and bones,
flesh and the scaffolding that lifts it.
Beauty and terror.
Bird into dog and dog into dirt.
Bird into dog and dog into dirt.

Verses of the Earth refrain:

All that lives
goes to die
All that dies
goes to feed
All that lives.

All that lives
goes to die
All that dies
goes to feed
All that lives.

All that lives
goes to die
All that dies
goes to feed
All that lives

Talking the Ears off the Stars

I have this house with a roof that leaks.
I have this yard that's eroding into the street.
I have this house that I don't really own
won't really own for 35 years
long past my retirement
long past my ability to pay.
I have this house that some bank
can yank out from under me like a slapstick carpet
anytime they want in the next 35 years.

But while I am here
I intend to sit in my chair
and read my books.
I intend to drink beer under the stars on my patio
and talk into the wee hours
talk the ears off the stars
talk until the moon nods and droops below the treeline
until the words spill down the street
and find their rivulet byways into the LA River
and perhaps at last to the sea.
I intend to pick my way up my outdoor cement staircase
and piss outside in the dark down into my gully.
I intend to invoke the possessive—*my*—over all these things
until and unless the law slams shut on my fingers.

I intend to crawl into bed far too late
nuzzle my sleeping wife
get nuzzled by my sleeping dogs
only to be tickled awake before dawn
by the whiskers of my cat on my face
to rise once more in this place
this decaying, beautiful place
this place where I have stopped for awhile
in my dizzy spin around this wobbly globe
as it fishtails its way through the firmament,
in my life's brief blink
of the universal eye.

The One-Turn Waltz

So strange
how the future
becomes the past

Skips
off the crest
of the present
Skims
into the past

Waltzes you one turn
for one
blistering glance
drops your hand

Spins into the past

Rest

To watch the hawk, on subtle wing
caress the face of the upturned sky
drift on the gusts of air that rise through the cove.

  Because he will not fall
  I can rest.

To watch the waves lunge
drum the cove, slap the rocks
massage down through crevasses.

  Because they will not stop
  I can rest.

To hear log knuckles crack
in the stone fireplace, see sheets of flame
snap like clothes on a line in a high wind.

  Because their hunger burns
  I can rest.

To see the surf churn and froth
swirl foam circles and break
in tail-flick snaking lines and dissolve

  Because it will not cease
  before my mortal eyes
  I can rest.

Things Wondrous Made of Plain Things

Our night opens on a sky of stars made
from rusty nails and screws spread
across a horizon wall at Future Studios.

Then it's on to MorYork where the labyrinth
beckons us through a mild-mannered front gallery
into a fantastical trove of assemblage art oddities
and museum of found-object storage.

Twisting aisles and alleyways through
bundles of doll parts mummified in cellophane
that dangle like surreal stalactites from the ceiling
and serpentine columns of nested bottle caps
that rise like bizarre stalagmites from the floor—
multi-headed they snake and grope for the rafters.

The sharp geometry of city towers architected
out of Scrabble tiles, raw materials in free stacks
and nestled in the drawers of apothecary chests
while straight rows of long, low display cases
filled with small animal skulls and bones
enforce a stubborn order along one wall.

Move closer then to the shining silver chairs and see
they're made of aluminum can pull-tabs and think
how can that be comfortable? But give them a try, sit,
feel their shocking springy give—how it calls you
in soft metallic whisper to settle in and stay, rest,
imagine, let your mind pick its way back through
all these things wondrous made of plain things.

Everything Alive Moving Makes a Sound

Redwood forest night dark
and I am an animal
in the mouth of my den.
I am the stupidest animal in the forest
who struggles to decode the simplest sounds
of the life that everywhere surrounds me
where nothing alive moving can be seen
and everything alive moving makes a sound.

I am the animal of the grand, clueless plan.
House-sitting for my absent friend, I fired up
some Hendrix, cracked a beer, opened the sliding glass door
and came out to sit on this deck awash
in light from the house, to admire and commune
with this redwood forest night dark.
But the dark stayed away. The redwood night
retreated from my assault.

I came to the lip of my bombastic den
which blasts light and thudding, screeching sounds
into the clearing and the wild night, well past my natural reach.
This shelter of my species projects its protective shell
like a porcupine's flared quills or a skunk's noxious fumes
to make me seem larger and more frightening
than my weak, pale, furless, clawless, and fangless native form.

On a platform of planks made from the bones of the forest
I sit on a dirty white seat fashioned from the liquid remains
of creatures millions of years dead, dredged up
out of deep pockets in the rock halfway around the world
from here in Mendocino, in Northern California,
up on this hill half a mile from the ocean.

The redwoods rise leafless stories tall,
spread their canopy to net the stars,
mask the moon and tamp down the dark,
which pools among the damp ferns and sorrel,
noses down into the red blanket of shed bark
and forest decay spread across their roots.
I am heretic in this prehistoric cathedral, untutored,
ignorant of the chirped hymns, murmured liturgy,
reverberant psalms of its congregants
everywhere hidden in these honeycombed halls
where everything alive moving makes a sound.

So first I turn off the music
to invite the forest sounds closer. Again I sit,
dullest and stupidest animal in the forest,
so slow on the uptake, before I rise again
to turn off every light in the house
and creep back out onto the deck.

Now at last my little den, dark and silent,
recedes into the forest at my back.
Even the sloshing and sipping of my beer
has become offensive, a trespass, so I set it aside
to listen, listen to the quiet alive
and watch, watch the patient dark.

Water drips on leaves. Small animal rustles brush.
Rodent? Snake? I don't even know what's out there.
Somewhere in this forest are foxes, deer.
Bears maybe? Even mountain lions? I am helpless to do
what even the least life form here must learn early
to survive—separate and know the sources
of the sounds that populate this world.
I find the tiniest creatures make the biggest noise—
insect twillings and chizzings over gradual minutes rise,
crash through the forest, crescendo and subside.

The longer we sit in darkness
the more penetrating our eyes become
and the longer we sit in quiet
the more discerning our ears.

In the background, the susurrous wind in the canopy.
Wind known, farther back and below the wind I can tease it out—
from past the edge of the redwood-crowned plateau,
over the crest and half a mile down—
the ocean. Its vast breast swells
all the way around the world, against every shore.
With the long inhale, slow exhale, the entire horizon
rises and falls, deep rumble in chest,
and I can hear the very earth breathing
because everything alive moving makes a sound.

Wordless

I drop my pen
and rise

draw a deep breath
and go

in
to the dim, the moist, the cool

the sun-laced and sun-speared
time-cradled forest

wordless
at last

Afterword: Every White Head Nodded

In April 2021, I took a class called Poems Are Where I Tell the Truth, taught by bridgette bianca over Zoom through Beyond Baroque, the literary arts center in Venice, California. As poet and author of *be/trouble*, bridgette is a brilliant, sharp, devastating yet always entertaining truth-teller. As a teacher she's generous, funny, thoroughly prepared but spontaneous, available to every student with all her wisdom and empathy.

So there I was in my little home office space set up for pandemic worklife, desk shoved against a window in the guest room with narrow clearance between the futon and a tall dresser. Stack of books on the dresser visible in my background. Lukewarm espresso on a coaster next to the keyboard. Dogs curled on the futon.

When bridgette, who is Black, asked the class, most of whom were white, for topics that we avoid in our writing, one poet mentioned wanting to write about her white privilege and the fears that stop her: she doesn't know how, every poem she's written about it is crap, maybe her voice isn't needed, she'll be judged. "I don't know how to write truth with this," she said.

"Look at that—and you shared it, and you did not melt immediately," bridgette answered with kind good humor. "So that was proof that you can do it. And it's not crap. That resonated with me, I can't even tell you."

I told the class that in the last couple years I'd been trying to write poetry that engages with race and whiteness in a way that's not bullshit. I talked about my own fears of getting it wrong.

Every white head on the screen nodded.

"My thesis has been that if I can do it with honesty, humility, and vulnerability, I can produce something that is worthwhile," I said. "I've had some false starts, and some things I think landed correctly, and I'm going to continue working on it."

bridgette offered only encouragement. "It's hard to do without feeling like bullshit and the reason why is because of course race is bullshit."

***

Race *is* bullshit. I think we can all agree on that.

Specifically, it's *white* bullshit. For four hundred years in this country, race has been used by people who look like me as the justification for pretty much the entire range of terrible things that one group of people can do to another.

Yet, when the thought really began to nag at me to finally tackle this aspect of life in my poetry, I too had a hard time convincing myself I had anything to say that someone else—namely, someone Black or brown—couldn't say better. And yes, I was terrified of the consequences of perhaps fucking it up. Much safer to keep writing my poems about Los Angeles freeways and people-watching, love, death, nature, my wife, and our cats.

But racism lives *inside* white people. We are its home. All of us born and raised here in the United States have a bit of it in us somewhere, don't we? It's not our fault, yet we're stuck with it. Our very brains were marinated in it. We probably hate it, might try to stuff it back down or deny it when one of those unprompted, unwilling racist thoughts bubbles up like a noxious sulfurous burp from a volcano, leaving that nasty little taste of lava in our mouths. We feel it, and it burns. But we know it's in there. We own that shit, whether we want to or not.

Maybe that makes us as white poets uniquely situated to address race and whiteness in our work.

***

With all that in mind, why did I decide to take this on?

Seeds were sown early. I still have a haunting memory of my parents, stunned and silent, watching Walter Cronkite report the assassination of Martin Luther King, Jr. in our basement family room in Kalamazoo, Michigan when I was five years old. King's murder galvanized them into the civil rights movement: my father a political science professor who taught classes on race in American politics; and my mom an archaeologist who somehow taught me without ever explicitly saying it that every human being who's ever lived in anytime anyplace any culture was just as real and alive, just as fully a person, as I am, as you are.

Early in those years I remember sitting on a hard metal folding chair in a high school gymnasium watching black-and-white footage of the Montgomery bus boycott, King preaching, vicious out-of-control white cops beating dignified Black marchers, blasting them with hoses, setting snarling dogs on them to rip their clothes and flesh, the white cops snarling just like their dogs. That footage hit me like a club. The bruise is still there. I knew who was right and who was wrong, and wrong lived in the ones who shared my skin color.

I remember being down in a different Michigan basement with a merry crew, adults and children alike, paint cans, blank placards and sticks arrayed atop a long table, all of us painting yard signs with slogans like "Fair Housing: Action Now." I remember crowded living rooms in Black neighborhoods, in white neighborhoods, in our own house, where every chair and couch was filled and people stood around, Black and white, all ages, voices deep and resonant, full of strategy and intensity.

On a separate track, my mom used to read to me every night before bed through much of my childhood. Most of those books had magic in them of some kind, and some had poetry: *A Child's Garden of Verses, East of the Sun and West of the Moon* (a book of fairy tales from all over the world), *Winnie-the-Pooh, The Wizard of Oz* (my great-grandfather invented the name Oz, but that's another tale for another time), Dr. Seuss, *The Hobbit* and *The Lord of the Rings.* Her voice and the texts she intoned wove a spell. Somehow something in me sensed the consciousness behind those spells, a kind of wizard: the writer. I wanted to learn how to weave magic with words like that.

I started writing poetry seriously in 1983, when I was 20 years old, the same year I moved to Los Angeles. But for the first thirty years here, I submitted and performed my work only sporadically. By late 2013, something built up inside me and finally burst, driving me out into the LA poetry scene—which had changed a lot since my earlier forays.

Much is simultaneity, not sequence, and context is everything. Trayvon Martin was murdered in 2012; Black Lives Matter founded in 2013; Eric Garner, Michael Brown, Ferguson, all 2014. None of this was new, of course. Only the impact of technology was new: the audio of 911 calls, the cell phone videos, how word spread on social media and brought white attention to the violence and horror. The movement branded our language with new incantations, a tragic poetry that memorialized lives lost: I can't breathe. Hands up, don't shoot. Black Lives Matter. Say their names.

As I came out onto the LA poetry scene in that era, the group I bonded with easiest at the time were poets like me who were largely unknown, first making the rounds of the open readings, seeing each other over and over out and about. Mostly, these were poets of color decades younger than me. We'd hang around afterward, talk, exchange information, and make friends later on Facebook.

We make words and phrases because we need them to describe the important features of our world. Apparently, Inuit don't really have fifty different words for snow but it's easy to imagine they would. The Facebook feeds of these younger friends of mine were full of phrases new to me or which I'd heard but didn't fully understand: ally, microaggression, gatekeepers, STFU and listen, callout, the only one in the room, white fragility, white tears, white nonsense, white fuckery, decolonization. For all the crimes we can legitimately lay at the feet of Facebook, Twitter, and other social media—and I notice it's mostly white folks taking that line—I've learned so freaking much in those spaces.

These younger BIPOC (Black, Indigenous, people of color) poets welcomed me, and I found myself drawn to their energy, urgency, spirit, and innovation. I've seen my friends engage and revitalize poetry and performance in Los Angeles in real time, building community in visionary ways and living the changes we need through poetry and the arts. I'm lucky to be here for that.

I saw that my friends did not shy away from addressing race in their work. It's the stuff of their lives—not something apart and abstract, merely "political" and disembodied.

I think one reason many white poets don't write about race is a learned reticence to write political poetry. Is this just a leftover modernist prejudice? "No ideas but in things?" Is it the culture of WASP reserve, our training that it's impolite to talk religion or politics? Or is it an active repression of awareness around race, racism, and the harm caused? A way to protect ourselves by turning our eyes elsewhere and then dignifying it as an aesthetic stance?

It's the stuff of our lives too, whether we choose or refuse to see. When we ignore or compartmentalize race as political and decide it's not worthy of art, we make an active decision to impoverish our own work, to rob it of dimension and consequence. Poetry is big enough to contain the whole world.

Many of the best BIPOC poets and writers talk about decolonizing their work, rejecting some of these white craft aesthetics. I began to wonder how—or if—I as a white poet, a descendant of colonizers, might be able to decolonize my own mind and work.

I also began to feel an obligation to my new BIPOC friends not to leave all this to them. To do my part, whatever that might be.

As I learned from Toni Morrison's short, brilliant book *Playing in the Dark: Whiteness and the Literary Imagination*, race has been the unacknowledged backdrop for all literature in this country. Black is the ground on which whiteness is defined. Our American obsession with freedom—in our politics, literature, and homegrown mythologies—arose during our first few centuries directly within the context of a massive population of enslaved Black people. Our archetypal American motif of the road, lighting out for the territories, by horse, by train, by fast car, can be seen as an obsession not just with freedom but escape. Tearing ourselves away, setting ourselves apart or above. But we really can't, can we?

After decades of being concerned with race in my politics and personal life, I began to ask myself: Where was it in the poetry?

The more I asked, the more it became a trick question.

Is it in the poetry? That was the real question. And the only possible answer was yes.

Either it's there because I put it there or it's there because I left it out. It's either a presence or a visible absence. A wound open to the air and healing or a festering abscess. To the extent I've ignored race in my poetry, whiteness is there. It's the privilege of my whiteness that allows me to ignore it. Once I saw that, I became responsible to what I saw.

And the notion that somehow art and poetry are above politics and race? I now see this as another idea of whiteness that protects whiteness.

***

Once our brains have been remapped in certain ways, we can sometimes faintly trace the old roads but we can never travel them again. As old as I was by this point—late forties through early fifties—and for as long as I'd been concerned with racial equality, the things I learned from my new friends of color in real life and on social media set my internal globe spinning.

Two great revelations came in 2015 out of the case of white conceptual poet Vanessa Place's project of tweeting out the entirety of the book *Gone With the Wind* one tweet at a time—with its many uses of the n-word intact and Hattie McDaniel as Mammy for a profile pic.

As a white liberal progressive intellectual, appreciator of John Cage and fan of John & Yoko's conceptual art activism, I immediately understood Place's project as an anti-racist provocation. BIPOC on the other hand roundly and unanimously denounced it as racist. There was no hesitation on this point, no debate—and I was completely befuddled by it.

It hurts to admit this in naked print, but *I* thought *they* just didn't get it. I had an urge to jump on Facebook threads and explain it to them. Now I see the unconscious racism in that thought and it pains me. But there's no growth without honest self-appraisal, and there it is.

What kept me from posting my arrogance? The terror of fucking up backed by the suspicion that perhaps it was actually *me* who didn't get it. Maybe there was something important I needed to understand and the best way to learn was to listen, search, study—question my own biases, as my father taught me—*before* I uttered a public word.

I read Place's artistic statement and listened to a podcast where she defended it. Something about courting a lawsuit from the Margaret Mitchell estate for copyright infringement, forcing them to defend *Gone With the Wind*'s racism in court. A brilliant conceptual stunt from a certain standpoint, it involved Place, also a lawyer, offering to step on a judicial cross as a kind of white liberal martyr.

I pondered every comment, every reply, in my friends' Facebook threads, read the Change.org petition created by an anonymous group called Mongrel Coalition Against Gringpo—and admired their conceptual guerilla activism as well. I tracked links from web point to web point and read all about it from multiple perspectives.

At some critical-mass juncture the revelation snapped into place and the cards flipped in my brain all down the line from face-down to face-up. I saw clearly what I couldn't see before and now I can never unsee it.

"Nothing about us, without us, is for us." That slogan on a poster by social activist artist Ricardo Levins Morales had stuck in my head and it helped me to understand.

I also learned about intention versus impact. Whites who offend BIPOC often resort to good intentions as defense, whereas BIPOC stress the very real and cumulative personal toll of harmful impacts and their resentment at being expected to repeatedly forgive the same rude behavior that white people are too self-centered to figure out not to commit. Example: white people wanting to touch Black hair. The white person might experience their own intention as harmless curiosity. For the Black person, it's invasive and rude and gets old fast.

Whatever Place's intentions, her project shot daily injections of racist language and narrative into the world—on purpose, by design. Black and brown people did not want to see the n-word, Mammy images, and the Southern lost-cause nostalgia of *Gone With the Wind* fouling up their Twitter feeds every day. They didn't need Vanessa Place to tell them it was racist or get her ass hauled into court to prove the obvious.

Her project was not for Black people. It was a cocky show-off stunt by a white liberal intellectual for status and credibility with other white liberal intellectuals who could admire—even envy—her bold conceptual brilliance but would not suffer daily pain from it. Insulated as she was in her academic cocoon, she seemed completely oblivious that anyone other than a white racist could possibly object.

Over and over we see this: white liberals, poets, actors, comedians, and celebrities get called out for writing or saying something hurtful and racist in impact, regardless of their intentions or simple cluelessness. I often see this as a misapprehension of audience on their part. These white people speak all-unknowing right past Black and brown people as if they don't exist to an unconsciously imagined white audience, a "we" that looks, talks, thinks, even jokes like them. As if that white-based "we" were the only audience worth addressing. The only ones who matter.

One of the privileges white people have long held without being aware of it—which is, of course, how privilege works—is the privilege to decide for the culture at large what racism is: who are the racists; what words, thoughts, and deeds shall be considered racist. We've held this privilege as the overwhelming cultural gatekeepers—or bouncers, as I picture it—standing at the velvet ropes and stanchions around the cultural main square, looking everyone up and down to decide who gets in, who has the right look, who gets tossed out for "inappropriate" behavior, and how long anybody stays. We've been the publishers, the editors, the university presidents and professors, the owners of broadcast networks, producers, talk show hosts, public intellectuals, most influential writers, major celebrities. Enforcing an unspoken quota for decades: no more than one to three Black voices allowed into the square at a time. And if we could get them to argue with each other for our entertainment, all the better: James Baldwin, MLK, Malcolm, a Black Panther or two, Toni Morrison, Al Sharpton, the occasional Black actor, a Sidney Poitier or Morgan Freeman. Always introduced, framed, explained, and summarized by the white host/authority. And naturally, such white gatekeepers—even liberal ones—have historically defined racism in favor of our own biases and perspectives.

But in these last ten years, social media and other aspects of the exponential growth in media outlets have seen BIPOC voices pushing past the bouncers, ducking under the ropes, knocking over the stanchions, claiming and holding space. Lo-and-behold and surprise, surprise to a lot of white folk accustomed to acclaiming each other enlightened, liberal, and progressive—BIPOC have their own ideas about what constitutes racism and effective allyship.

Now that I see this, I never want to write past my BIPOC friends and others I don't know toward some insular, white audience who calls itself "we" and believes itself representative. No more. This is not what we should be doing. This is committing a kind of careless violence with words, ignorant of who we might hurt.

***

Do white people even have the right to write about race? Is our perspective unavoidably clouded, inherently suspect? Let's reframe the question. When we think about race, don't we think about Black people? In this culture, Black people are raced. White people are neutral, default. Raceless.

Rather than naming the subject as race—which makes it a Black problem—let's call it whiteness. When we look at it that way the answer becomes clear. Who is better qualified to write about whiteness than white people?

When my dad got active in the civil rights movement after King was killed, he sought counsel from Black friends. He asked how he could help. They said they had the Black community covered. They needed him in the white community. That's where change had to occur.

What feelings are present in our hearts and what thoughts in our heads specifically, uniquely, because we are white? What experiences have we had around race? What gave us the belief we can't touch it? That's whiteness. That's where we live and it's ours to explore.

We can support and be allies, even accomplices, to our Black and brown sisters and brothers. We can use our privilege to amplify their voices. But we can't speak for them. And we should not speak over them.

We can speak from the white mind to the white mind and for the white mind. It's the white mind that needs to change. That's the tough and necessary work only we can do.

Historically, white writers and poets have largely ducked this. If we bump into race, we jump back, walk around it, hold a tender pink hand up to shield our faces like a child trying to make something scary disappear.

This seems fundamentally unfair to me—for white poets to hunker down in this privilege and leave our Black and brown sisters and brothers to shoulder the burden alone.

How do we bring that into our conscious awareness so it becomes available to us to deepen and enrich our poetry? How do we create work that doesn't seem to believe it exists in an all-white world—pitched to an all-white audience?

I don't have the answers. I write these poems to explore the questions.

***

I'm also clear that the risks I face as a white poet poetizing about whiteness are nothing next to the risks faced by Black and brown human beings merely trying to live and thrive in the world. As white people, the risks we take are circumscribed by our privilege.

I'm willing to chance writing something problematic without meaning to and getting called out for it. I've been called out before and I'm grateful. In one case, it was done privately by a dear friend with such loving kindness that my heart swells to think about it. Next time it might hurt like hell. But I'll still learn from it. I embrace that risk to do the work. Sometimes I might get it wrong, but I've got to try, because if white people aren't talking and writing about racism, then we all just keep on going as we have been, and we know that's not working. Something has to change. That something is likely us.

For many of us white folk who consider ourselves liberal, progressive, anti-racist, these stances live at the core of our self-identity. Studies show that in certain primal parts of our brain an attack on one's self-concept registers as a literal threat to our lives. The idea that we might be misconstrued, get named racist in some way can be terrifying. It feels in our place of irrational fears like we could die. Like our career, reputation, friendships, could be torn limb from limb, drawn and quartered.

The reality is closer to this: Our whiteness is a kind of magical forcefield that surrounds us and makes our way easier in the world, softens most blows and frequently bounces real consequences right off. What do we do with our privilege?

I believe the proper response to a callout is to receive it with humility. Listen closely, take in the lesson, sit with whatever feelings it provokes of hurt, defensiveness, fragility. Don't respond publicly out of those raw feelings, but cradle them, gentle them. Digest and process. If it helps, find a close, trusted, white friend to share them. Do not burden a Black or brown friend with this stuff. If an apology is called for, make it thoughtful, vulnerable, and real.

That's how we learn. That's how we grow.

***

We come, at last, to the poems themselves. I only have four to show for my efforts so far—minus the misfires, false starts, and incompletes. That's okay, the work continues. All four are in this book: "Systemic Pandemic," "Mark, Hank Aaron, and the Skinny Honky," "The One You Can't See in the Dark," and "The White Liberal Poet Organizes a Reading Against Racism." It's not for me to say the extent to which any of them succeed, fail, or fall in between.

I started small. I began by brainstorming every memory I could find that had anything at all to do with race. That's how I wrote the two poems about Black friends in my childhood and high school: Mark and Charlie.

In "Mark, Hank Aaron, and the Skinny Honkey," I took a memory from one era of my life to build a portrait of a time and place in this country, how white children were not taught to view Black children as full human beings. Just one memory, which I attempted to recall in as much telling detail as I could.

"The One You Can't See in the Dark" also began in one nagging memory which changed the more I worked it, until at last I understood what it had to show. It too grew into a specific portrait of a time and place. An anatomy of what we'd now call a micro-aggression, how it looked and felt from inside the one committing it. Letting go at last of my self-justifications, while not harping on my guilt. How a sincere, well-meaning white dude who does not see himself as racist can still make a friend feel like a stranger.

The evolution of that poem was a lesson for me. I performed an earlier draft to a small crowd that turned out to be mostly white. The poem went over big. Rousing applause, very well-received, and I was pleased with myself. My wife, perhaps my most insightful critic, had another take.

"Just because an audience full of white people liked the poem," she said, "doesn't mean it's finished." Then she pointed to a couple elements she found problematic: a long section where I jumped into Charlie's head and assumed his point of view, including a metaphor of a prison yard where he's surrounded by guns pointed at him from guard towers, which Elise felt had unfortunate and unnecessary connotations.

If you remember the poem, you can see how I went back and addressed the two concerns. The part where I empathize with Charlie is shorter now, and I'm in my own head, not his, attempting to see the situation as he might have experienced it. There's no prison yard metaphor and the guns became white teeth. I've also now workshopped the poem with Black and brown classmates and performed it before majority-BIPOC audiences.

Even in "Communal Best," a poem that's not directly about race, I chose to describe each of the people I saw in this public place with their ethnicity, to acknowledge it as part of the tapestry of urban life. In reality, in life, I see it—so I wrote about it. I didn't leave it out of the poem, pretend not to see what's right in front of me and flatten that dimension from the landscape.

If a character's race is not identified, they're conventionally assumed to be white. In a metropolitan area like Los Angeles, which is around 25% white, that's a glaring numerical falsehood. The absence of even the slightest acknowledgement of race becomes a lurking, looming presence. This is one more thing for us to play with and question as poets.

***

Key to this work for me are a few principles:

1. I must do the work myself, by which I mean: my own introspection into my own whiteness—my thoughts, feelings, experiences around race; being honest with myself about them, and seeking to understand.

2. I read, study, and listen—*really listen*—to BIPOC voices, to understand as much as I can of their experiences and points of view and how they differ from mine.

3. I try never to ventriloquize a BIPOC voice or take on a BIPOC persona. For me, this work is about owning and exploring whiteness.

4. I don't ask BIPOC to do my work for me. I've heard too many BIPOC accounts of white people—sometimes friends, sometimes mere acquaintances—asking BIPOC to vet or approve their work without performing their own due diligence. I never want to put my friends in that position. If the help is mutual and arises organically, that's a different story. That's friendship, not using.

5. I do seek to put the work to a fair test where it's open to BIPOC callouts and where I know I'll get an unvarnished, honest reaction. This means, again, the situation must be organic and mutual. As I write this, I'm in a majority-BIPOC poetry class with a workshop component. Still, I didn't lead with the material involving race. I had plenty of other poems to work on too. First we built a solid foundation of trust and respect—a community of friends and colleagues who knew we had each other's backs and could speak frankly.

***

It seems to me that the real work of dismantling racism has to be done where we live. It's not just demanding that Hollywood, politicians, and corporate executives change. As poets, we live in poetry. We come alive on the page and at the mic. We make family in the community of other poets. How do we enact change in our own family? How do we address what our whiteness does in the world?

Racism might not be our fault, but once we see it, it becomes our responsibility to act on what we've seen. If we don't, then maybe from that point on it is our fault.

If we produce or join in readings, performances, panels, are they all or mostly white? Why? Is it just easier that way? Could we do a little work to make the balance better reflect the demographics of where we live? Or even extend past that balance? Without tokenizing anyone? Let's never set up our BIPOC friends and colleagues to be the Only One in the Room.

Let's read, find community with, and amplify writers of color. Let's learn when to use our voice and when to let it fall silent, the better to listen. In Black and brown spaces, we can learn far more this way, and it's the best way to show our solidarity and respect.

I suggest we figure out how to write all of it, even the fears and questions. Put it to incidents, images, and metaphor. Give it word music.

There is poetry here and it's our job to find it. We're poets.

***

> *"[White people] are, in effect, still trapped in a history which they do not understand; and until they understand it, they cannot be released from it...Many of them, indeed, know better, but, as you will discover, people find it very difficult to act on what they know. To act is to be committed, and to be committed is to be in danger."*
>
> —James Baldwin, *The Fire Next Time*

***

Books that specifically informed my thinking here:

- *Playing in the Dark: Whiteness and the Literary Imagination* by Toni Morrison
- *Notes of a Native Son* and *The Fire Next Time* by James Baldwin
- *White Flights: Race, Fiction, and the American Imagination* by Jess Row
- *A Sense of Regard: Essays on Poetry and Race*, edited by Laura McCullough
- *The Racial Imaginary: Writers on Race in the Life of the Mind*, edited by Claudia Rankine, Beth Loffreda, and Max King Cap

Poem Notes

- Systemic Pandemic: the small California town is Los Alamos, north of Santa Barbara.
- Years Within Years (Nahuatl New Year, El Sereno): the cafe was Xocolatl Café in El Sereno, CA.
- LA Freeway Songbook | On the Braided River: describes driving the 210 west from San Dimas toward Los Angeles with the San Gabriel Mountains on the right (north).
- Mark, Hank Aaron, and the Skinny Honky: the documentary my mom took me to see is most likely *King: From Montgomery to Memphis* shown as a one-time event on March 24, 1970.
- Mind Full Suite: *The Miracle of Mindfulness* is by Thich Nhat Hanh. The phrase "present moment, wonderful moment," is from a Thich Nhat Hanh meditation.
- Coffee: written April 8, 1993, in San Francisco, as a collaboration on typewriter with poet and writer Scott Roat. His friend Bethany chose the title. Scott then wrote the first couple of lines and we traded off roughly one to three lines each to the end. No revisions have been made to that first draft except for a few bits of punctuation.
- Halfway There (Airport Poem): the trusty paperback is *Alpha Centauri or Die!* by Leigh Brackett (Ace Books). The spirits were Johnny Walker Black.
- Carry Me Off to Breakfast: allusions to Paul Simon and Art Garfunkel in reference to their song "Punky's Dilemma" from the album *Bookends*. Nod to John Lennon for his books of nonsense poetry *In His Own Write* and *A Spaniard in the Works*.
- Blogger Old Potatoes: probably written in 1985, giving the word blogger its first meaning as the nonsense curse word of a two-or-so-year-old girl. Scott Roat published the poem online in 1992 at worldmind.com in a section of nonsense pieces. He called the section "Bloggers," giving the word its second meaning: a nonsense word meaning nonsense. According to Wikipedia, the word's present usage was coined in about 1999 by Evan Williams for a web log software called Blogger from Pyra Labs. On September 1, 1999, the day the software was released, one of the developers, Paul Bausch, posted the second stanza of the poem on his blog "On Focus."

One can imagine him entering the word in a search engine on that day to find references to his software and unexpectedly finding the poem on Scott's site. Somewhat ironically, as a blogger (current, widely accepted definition), I blogged this history in more depth for my "Hippie Squared" feature on Ernessa T. Carter's Fierce and Nerdy blog: https://fierceandnerdy.com/hippie-squared-blogger-old-potatoes

- The White Liberal Poet…: the poem title *Horseshit Highway Manifesto* is an ironic riff on the title *Blood Highway Manifesto* by C. Natale Peditto, though the poet is not based on Chris, who was a model for me of authentic allyship. Mike the Poet Sonksen (first introduced to me by Chris), also a model for me of white allyship, appears with his kind permission and as a counter-example to the fictional poets depicted. The phrase "making a catastrophe of his own feelings" comes from Jess Row in his book *White Flights: Race, Fiction, and the American Imagination.*

- Mom Laughs: the book I bought on her birthday was *Agincourt: Henry V and the Battle That Made England* by Juliet Barker (Back Bay Books, 2008).

- COVID Killer Blues: a recorded version of this song is available on iTunes and several other musical platforms with "LefthandedJeff" as the artist name. Music, guitar, and voice on that version are by Justin Beauchamp. Links here: www.lefthandedjeff.com/covidkillerblues

- End Sea Begin Sky: Muir Woods on LSD circa 1995.

- Freeing the Balloons: the clown on the window was Ronald McDonald, the old McDonald's mascot. The store was on Santa Monica Boulevard near Beverly Glen. Someone rented the whole front part of the restaurant for a kid's private birthday party, while the drive-thru remained open to regular customers.

- Bleak LA: the movie theater was the old Rialto Theater on Fair Oaks in Pasadena.

- Quandary of the Beloved: the restaurant was Palermo on Vermont Avenue in Los Feliz, Los Angeles.

- Walked Up From Sunset: the bus stop was on Franklin (north side) at Hillhurst in Los Angeles.

- Car Stereo Jukebox: the Neil Young song was "Cinnamon Girl."

- Time Sings the Universe: inspired by a book review of *The Fabric of the Cosmos: Space, Time, and the Texture of Reality* by physicist Brian Greene, called "Space and time, strings attached," written by K.C. Cole and published in the Los Angeles Times on March 7, 2004.

- Rest: Little River Inn, Little River, CA, near Mendocino, where I proposed to my wife in 1996.
- Things Wondrous Made of Plain Things: Artist Nan Wollman made the stars of rusty nails and screws: https://wollmanstudios.com/. The galleries Future Studios and MorYork are in Highland Park in Los Angeles. MorYork and all its assemblage art are the works of Clare Graham: https://moryork.com/

Publication Acknowledgements

Thank you to the editors, publishers, and staff of the following publications who published versions of these poems in print or online:

- *Acid Verse: the Earth Beneath Our Feet* (Los Angeles Poet Society Press): "This Body Me"
- *Altadena Poetry Review: Anthology 2016* (Golden Foothills Press): "Fed the Dogs Tune" and "Milk Jar Ditty" (as "Milk Jar Tune")
- *Altar Collective Volume VIII*: "New Friend in Los Angeles"
- *Archive 405*: "Time Sings the Universe" (as "Time"), "Time Blossoms," and "Wordless"
- *Capital and Main: Words of Fire*: "An LA Freeway Songbook"
- *The Coiled Serpent: Poets Arising From the Cultural Quakes & Shifts of Los Angeles* (Tia Chucha Press, 2016): "LA Freeway Songbook" and "What Grows Below Ground"
- *Cultural Daily* (culturaldaily.com): "The White Liberal Poet Organizes a Reading Against Racism"
- *Direction '95* (Los Angeles Pierce College): "Coffee" and "Elegy to the Mystic Poet" (as "Woulds: Elegy")
- *Direction '96* (Los Angeles Pierce College): "Quicksand Mirror" and "Walked Up From Sunset"
- *Dryland Lit*: "Mission of San Juan Capistrano Ruins"
- *Fierce and Nerdy* (fierceandnerdy.com): Many of the poems in this book began life or appeared here on Ernessa T. Carter's blog site as part of my "Hippie Squared" and "Three Line Lunch" sections.
- *Hominy, Vol. 1*: "Coffee"
- *Journal of Modern Poetry (JOMP) 19: Poetry of Protest*: "Give Me Questions"
- *Journal of Modern Poetry (JOMP) 20: The Poetry Writer's Guide to the Galaxy*: "In Spaceships"
- *LA Art News* (laartnews.com/poetsplace): "Things Wondrous Made of Plain Things"

- *Los Angeles 1956 #1*: "Carry Me Off to Breakfast"
- *Los Angeles 1956 #2*: "Blogger Old Potatoes"
- *Los Angeles 1956 #4*: "Connective Tissue"
- *NELA Art News*: "What Grows Below Ground"
- *Public Intellectuals* (publicintellectuals.org): "Mark, Hank Aaron, and the Skinny Honky" (with illustration by publisher Teka Lark)
- *Spectrum: 140 SoCal Poets*: "Homunculus Highway Brain Burrito"
- *Spectrum 2*: *The Gift:* "Walked Up From Sunset"
- *Spectrum 5: Every Poem is an Idea*: "Freeing the Balloons"
- voces / voices of the poets (avenue50studio.org/voces-of-the-people): "Give Me Questions"
- *Worldmind* (worldmind.com): "Carry Me Off to Breakfast" and "Blogger Old Potatoes"
- The poem "What Grows Below Ground" was a poetry contest winner for Lummis Day 2015 and was printed as a broadside and a postcard by the Los Angeles Department of Cultural Affairs
- The poem "Coffee" hung on the wall of The Depot Café & Bookstore in Mill Valley, CA in the 1990s and in 2014 it hung on the wall of Coffee Klatch in San Dimas, CA.
- The poems "A Lover's Map" and "Heart Tectonics" were printed as postcards by Linda Kaye Poetry for Valentines Day 2015.

Personal Acknowledgements

This book is the celebration of a lifetime—multiple lifetimes, it feels like. Its birthday is December 3, 2022. Two days later I turn sixty.

So I have these lifetimes of gratitude to shoehorn into these next few pages. I fear they won't contain it. If your copy of the book bulges out at this section, you know why: I couldn't quite stuff it all in.

Everything I've ever known, felt, experienced, and imagined, is somewhere in the pages of this book. That's the alchemy of art. All the best, worst, and in-between of me is in it. I believe that every least interaction I've ever had with any human being has shaped me in some indiscernible way and its all here in the ore, in the veins and seams, hiding under the crook of an r, dancing on the head of an i, dangling off the foot of an L.

Thank you, everyone, for all of it.

Especially those whose names I never knew, who didn't know mine, who will never read these words. Thank you for the unknown part you played.

Thank you to those whose names should be here but for whatever reason I've overlooked. If you believe you should be in here and you aren't, you are no doubt right. I've probably noticed by now and your absence may well haunt me. Please accept my apologies and my thank you.

***

Though I've already dedicated the book to them and they've passed into the part of life that feeds the living, I still need to give first thanks to my parents, Margaret (Peggy) Anne Bishop Rogers Holman: Mom. And Chester Benjamin Rogers: Dad. I'm equal parts you and some mysterious third thing and I'm grateful for the whole mix. You gave me so much.

Elise Rodriguez, though I've already dedicated the book to you also, the next thank you still belongs to you. On St. Patrick's Day, 1994, I walked into your room. There you stood in the center of it. You turned toward me and I saw it all in your eyes. I fell in. I never stopped falling. On July 4, 1995, you moved in: Interdependence Day. We missed the hat trick of pegging anniversaries to major holidays when we married the day *after* Thanksgiving in 2005. You're my best friend, my favorite person to talk to, laugh with, walk dogs and snuggle cats with, and otherwise adventure with. Your laugh is my favorite song. When you left San Francisco for Los Angeles you knew if you met a man who loved Brautigan he'd be your man and you were right. Because of your confidence and loving push I won a job and made a career as a writer despite my lack of a college degree or any other credentials besides talent and intelligence. You believed that was enough when I was skeptical and your belief conjured my reality and a whole new life.

Because this is a book, the next thank you must go to my grandfather Clive Bishop. Elise and I would have named a son for him. He loved books and encouraged my dream of being a writer. His gentleness, humor, and wisdom were a constant and quiet example to me of how to be a human being in this world. In so many ways I followed in his footsteps without even knowing it.

Thank you to the rest of my Bishop family, especially my cousins Kathy, Holly, and Tizzy. How we famously did laugh, play, and make a mess. Thank you to Uncle Bob (gone now) and Aunt Lois.

Neither of my parents ever had any other children of their own. I was an only child until I was ten. So the next thank you goes to Fritz Cramer, my first friend, the closest I ever had to a blood brother. On Junedale Drive in Kalamazoo, Michigan, you were playing popsicle stick boats in the mud puddle of our driveway the day my parents and I moved into our house. You and I were three, in our 1965 crew cuts and shorts. But you marched up to me, stuck out your hand, and said, "Let's be friends." We played together nearly every day for the next seven years, until I moved away at ten. Your mischief and imagination helped shape me as a rebel and spinner of stories. You were my first friend, you set the pattern, and you will always be my longest friend, because we will always be friends.

To the rest of the Cramers and the whole world of Junedale Drive: Rob Vall, Carl Horner, the Birches, the Kramers.

To Liam Taylor in Evanston, Illinois. You taught me how to give bear hugs when you were 12 and I must have been around four. I idolized you and 12 became my favorite number.

To my first girlfriend and my first big unrequited love: Donna Hartman and Judy Clark, respectively. Both in kindergarten, Indian Prairie Elementary School. To all my friends there. To Miss Smelter, third grade teacher. To my friends at Westwood Elementary, also in Kalamazoo.

To the archaeologists: the crews of the Hangar and Camp Rondo in the summers of 1973, 1974, and 1975, and my mom's colleagues at the MSU museum and in the department. Those summers in the woods with crews of hippie archaeologists were such an adventure for me. They opened up the world. Sally, I wish I knew your last name, but I remember walking with you to the lake. Jan Brashler, Bill Lovis, Libby Bogdan, Kathy Bogdan, Pat and Susan Martin, Herb and Patty Whitier. George and Deb Sabo, Virgil Noble, Jim Brown, all the rest.

To the Holman Tribe: When I was eleven in 1974 my mom married Dr. J. Alan Holman. I gained stepbrothers: Joe, Ray, and Michael. We called our stitched-together family the Holman Tribe. Ray, you've been a true brother ever since. We grew up together. Streaked across Bailey Elementary, stayed up late to make scrambled eggs and watch *Twilight Zone, Kolchack: The Night Stalker* and the very first *Saturday Night Lives*, and walked from 540 Linden across the snowy Michigan State campus to see Magic Johnson play at Jenison Fieldhouse. All the stories and reminiscences, our personal legends, from Rondo to Jenison to Pinks and Lucy's El Adobe, and points in-between. Keep holding onto those Marvel Slurpee cups for us. To Erica and Hadley Rae Holman. To Michael: you owned downtown East Lansing as a charismatic urchin and I still remember the beauty of your signs at my kitchen table in Los Angeles when you visited. To April and your children.

To David Church: I love you, brother, and always will. We met in sixth grade. All the hours of talk after school; throwing the frisbee and football. Star Trek, beers, Beatles, Zeppelin in the basement. You were my longest best friend and your phone number from those days is long gone but still memorialized in many a PIN of mine. Living together in L.A. and Van Nuys. The times I called you to Don Antonio to share my latest revelations. You listened and always understood.

To John Mattson, my first writing partner, because this is a book, and for your friendship and partnership—for That Silent Sea, More About Penguins, Mother Flucker's, and The Spy from Russia Who Loved Me Twice With a Golden Gun. For drilling me mercilessly in how to tell one Beatle voice from another. I dreamed of being a writer before I met you in middle school at Curious Books and you launched a hostile takeover of my comic book company. But from there we built that dream together as writing partners, sometimes sentence-by-sentence and joke-by-joke, sometimes separately but side-by-side, and I'll never know how far I would have taken that dream on my own. On September 16, 1983, we loaded it up in the rust-fringed Chevy Malibu with our typewriters, crates of records, and boxes of books, and drove it across country from Michigan to LA. It has carried us both everywhere we've gone since. 400 billion cows can't be wrong and what are you doing with that parmesan cheese tapping rhythm in the hallway?

Frank Breen III, you saved me in high school because you didn't know I was a nerd. You saw the mellow, easygoing guy in me; I became what you saw and was socially redeemed. With Church and Mattson we were the Fab Four. Watched movies in your basement theater and drank way too much Mountain Dew.

Other Lansing, East Lansing, and Michigan friends, each important in their own way, from Lansing Avenue, Willow Street School, Hannah Middle School, East Lansing High School, Ponderosa Steakhouse: especially Valerie, Joel, and

Jeff; John Rux; Diego Bonesatti, Lee Irish—Frish forever, John Munro, Wayne Chen, Maggie Church, Lee Pritchard (first editor), Janine Hall Oberstadt (friend and early booster), Leah Popowski, Joan Potter, Irene Yen, Paula Worby, Mauri Ingram, Sonia Suter, Jay and Laura Reinbold (close, loving friends and supporters for decades, E.L. and Los Angeles family), Diana Price, Debbie Golob/Qory, Brad Goode, Carin Walter, Andy Sinadinos; Karen Horstman, Kendra McCourt, Colleen Tabor, Karen Otstot, Deirdre, and Charlie; Liz Little.

Cincinnati: To Scott Roat, "The Guy With the Purple Hat On," also because this is a book, and for your decades of close friendship. For Fosdick refuge, all the books we have in common, that meatball sandwich, for naming your nonsense page Bloggers, for Riley ripping up the door of my car, for Mendocino redwood refuge, for your generous ear. The Liggetts: Uncle Den, Aunt Rita, Greg; Joy Westfall; Sanders Hall 8th floor roommate Pat Prendergast who gave me Little Feat and Buffet, our suitemates, Scott Skinner.

Early LA years: To Tanja Barnes, my first real friend in Los Angeles, for Canter's, Bodhi Tree, Capote, Prince, the screenplay we nearly wrote and for putting me in your podcast. To Jeff Clem, second LA friend, where are you? Doug Nathan, long-suffering, tolerant roommate; David Martin, all the conversations examining intimate details of daily life, priceless—wish I knew how to find you; the Irish lads and lasses; Alfa Villaflor, Tonye Dockery. I wish I remembered his name, but when I opened at McDonald's on Santa Monica Blvd near Beverly Glen I'd get there early, sun not even up, and he'd be there dozing in his car. He spoke little English, I spoke little Spanish, but he'd open the passenger door and invite me to snooze beside him for a precious ten minutes before opening. He was a friend. Ava Bubly.

Crown Books: Shawn Hayden, next real LA friend and boon companion for movies, music, books, and more; Sandy Rojas, Erik Hanson, Arne Sundt, Susan Nelson, Jackie, Vanessa on Patricia Ave., John Lisi, Daryl O'Connor, Kevin Dooley. Daniel Carlson—I don't have to say a thing because you know and no matter how much time passes we just fall right into that old friends rhythm. Angus McIntosh—you made Los Angeles my home at last, probed Zen, Tai Chi, and the Tao with me, fixed me up with a girlfriend, then stole her away and married her; Nina McIntosh, Sharon McIntosh; Denise Grimes—Beatlefest forever.

Meeting Mira-Lani Perlman in April, 1986, was one of the great hinge points of my life. To Lani: you brought me into the poetry, writing, performance, and arts scene in Los Angeles, gave me a community of friends who embraced and sustained me for twenty years; featured me in my first poetry reading at Cloisters; pulled me into every mad genius project: BASFAP, YPL, Art Options, Ginger

Sverlo. I would not have met Elise had I not known you first, because the chain of connection led through you to Chris Peditto and Gray Pony, which led to Kimberley, whose new roommate Elise in 1994 happened to become the love of my life.

Important others from this circle and era: Steve Oglesby, hermit artist wiseman jester. Roland Starkey aka Santa Fish, I cannot thank you enough for your years of dry wit and warm and writerly friendship; Circling back to Chris Peditto, departed but immortal poet and founder of Gray Pony, friend, mentor, mesmerizing talker, a jazz monologist, erudite blower of cascading runs of words, scholar of the oral tradition, the Beats, bohemias worldwide, an early model for me of allyship and building community through poetry; Barbara Romain, dear friend of decades; Shelley Sachs—your love, wit, and friendship mean everything; Kimberley Edwards, wisewoman and friend of a lifetime; Harold Abramowitz; Jen Carruthers—longtime touchstone—Patty Malkin, Rich Ferguson, Tony Clay—the mystic poet died young—Tommy Chiffon, Mutahar Williams, Blaine and Rachel Steele, Lisa Papineau, Priscilla Huddleston; Robert Prior, genius MC for a theater of the wild mind; Connie Rivera—forever Salome—your husband Anthony and daughter Paloma Macias; Tony and Jon Torn. All the other Gray Ponies. Charles Bivins, the late Haight-Ashbury Falstaff bard. Elliott Levin, Justin Romain. Eric Brown, Karla Garcia, Shelly Rae Estes; Carey Fosse—all those parties where I felt like an alien until I found you and then I could relax.

In 1985 my dad married Elise Jorgens and I gained stepsisters Cat and Lis. Talking late into the night of the day we first met, the eve of our parents' wedding, we cemented the bond and we've been family ever since. Miko and Jackson, Chris and Genevieve, you round it all out. Elise Jorgens (Elise Sr., as we called you after my Elise came along): Family Forever. Thank you for the example you and my dad gave me of marriage as a true friendship and partnership.

To Paul and Dorie Rodriguez, you're my California family. I'm grateful for you and always feel at home when we're together. To all the other Rodriguezes: Joshua, Seth, Gabe, and Tabitha, and your children, thank you for being my extended family.

Time accelerates and I long to thank everyone but I know I can't. I've lived many lives, belonged to many communities. To my friends at Landmark Systems, especially Benita Sumbry, Terri Littlejohn, Andrea Moore, Bill Denise, Roz Bryant, Virgil, Chris; Young Playwrights Lab at Los Angeles Theater Center in the late eighties/early nineties; McCrusties: Mira-lani, Eric Brown, Andy Thomas, Randy Montano, Elizabeth Kadetsky, Tanya Ward Goodman, Rolly—again, ever, wherever and always.

Jewish Federation and AFSCME Local 800: especially Anju, Kumi, and all the extended Vyas family, who welcomed me with such warmth; Jacqueline Levian and our time together; Robert Haberman and Jacob Shavit—I think of you always together—the friendship, regard, respect, confidence you showed in me, all the hours of political and philosophical debate. The whole IT department: for 16 years we were family and then you gave me a laptop to write on when I left. Jan Greene—my work big sister, Ayala Cohavy—longtime officemate, lovely Agnessa Lifits, Dale Foster, Ilan Buchris; Mark Siegel, friend and mentor in the union writing game; Andrea Houtman, who alerted me to what became my first professional writing job. All my other friends from the JFC, Local 800, and Council 36, like Michael Quinn and Cheryl Parisi.

To Julie Butcher, another major hinge-point in my life—we hit it off at first meeting and you gave me my first writing job on pure instinct (and yes, my long hair had something to do with it), you backed me through some storms and always stuck with me. Jason Elias, brother from jump; Renee Anderson; Jenny Yang—I find the writers wherever I go; Simboa Wright; Rob Penney, you brought me into my next great writing job, where I still thrive.

Speaking of UNAC/UHCP: to my UNAC/UHCP Comms Department family—tight knit, infinitely supportive, we carried each other through COVID, and all the babies and cats on Zoom helped: Christy McConville, boss, friend, constant supporter; Russell Miller, Linda Sin—my work sister on the late shift, Anjetta McQueen Thackeray, true partner on press; Jashua Bane, Karin Mak; other UNAC family: Denise Duncan, RN, who asked me to edit and write a chapter of a book; Charmaine Morales, RN, "impactful words"; Peter Sidhu, RN; Bill and Nancy Rouse; Jeremy Lanni; somehow I always hit it off with the lawyers: Lisa Demidovich, Richa Amar, Jason Wojciechowski, Pamela Chandran, Jun Lim; Kuusela Hilo, Debra Sung, Richard Leon, Mandy Hartz.

Cypress Park/Mt. Washington: To the neighborhood watch of two decades standing, excellent neighbors all: Joy Cohen, neighborhood crier during the pandemic, Neale Aslett, Vishaal Khanna—close friend for so long now and how the hell did all that time pile up into the present? Stephanie Costanzo and mom Athena, Fatima Harmi, Tana Tyler Hamilton.

Writing Pad: To Marilyn Friedman and Jeff Bernstein, other teachers, mentors, friends: Amy and Seen Robinson, Lyn Gaza and Michael Manning, Tim Grierson, Steven Peros, Jon Davis, Ron Koertge, Amelia Gray, Ben Loory, Natasha Wang, Susan Howard—"nice shoes"—and Brandy Black; Douglas Wood; Angela Austin; Ernessa T. Carter—you invited me to join Fierce and Nerdy, dubbed me Hippie Squared—so I became a blogger two decades after inventing the word (different meaning, well sure)—and welcomed my Three Line Lunch project. To Eric Sims, good friend, mensch, brilliant comic writer, book club maestro, Beenandgoing where you invited me to be LefthandedJeff—happy to drive you home anytime, then idle at the curb and keep on talking as long as you want; to Lauren Mieger Sims. My other friends from the blogs and the Book Club for Dudes. The men's group: Mark Siegel (again), Gary Friedman, Elisha Shapiro, Michael Goldstein, Michael Alexander, Yadi Hashemi. Film Noir Club.

Michelle Sabol, I don't know how to express how much you've meant to the family that Elise and I have made together: her closest friend and one of my deepest. All the psychic, creative, emotional touchpoints. All the freaking uproarious doubled-over laughter together. To Kathy and Mary Sabol.

To Melanie Havelin: going on something like thirty years since we came to your party on the wrong night and you let us in anyway and made cocktails; and the talk, laughter, parties, politics, holidays, almond rocha, movies, ever-spreading friendship networks, ever since, have all meant more than I can say.

To Linda Kaye: you brought me into your poetry productions, embraced me, featured me often, and brought me so many friendships; Les Kaye, Jim Bolt, Lisa Montagne, Julio Rodriguez (the Conga Poet), others.

I love Los Angeles and a big part of my love for this place is the depth, breadth, warmth and strength of the poetry and arts community here with all its sub-communities and big-city small-world, way-overlapping Venn-mapped cross-pollinations. To all my friends, teachers, mentors, comrades, in this community. Especially the Writ Large, 90x90, Drunken Masters network, centered around Peter Woods, Chiwan Choi, and Judeth Oden Choi of Writ Large Projects. I love you and thank you for letting me be a part of your visionary acts of community-building. To Janine Lim, my beloved close partner in Drunken Masters. To Rocio Carlos and Ana Chaidez, how I love, admire, adore, and respect you both, separately and together. To Terry Robinson—like a brother from first meeting; bridgette bianca and Sara Borjas—two of the best poets on Earth, and here I am, so lucky to have you as friends to learn from up close; Armond Kinard, Luivette Resto, Teka Lark, Mike the Poet Sonksen, Kate Maruyama, Tiffany Hobbs, Jennifer Brody, Natashia Deon, Traci Akemi Kato-Kiriyama, so many more. To Laurel Ann Bogen, longtime Los Angeles master-poet and teacher, for your years of careful, patient, lessons, mentorship, friendship, and my mates in your classes: Marie Chambers, Jeff Rochlin, Mitchell Untch. To Steve Goldman for that early feature at Beyond Baroque. To Mike Mollett—brilliant artist, poet, taffy-limbed performer, Doug Knott. All the lefthanded Write Left poets and writers, starting with friend S.A. Griffin, who founded it, named it, and roped me in as co-founder: including Ellyn Maybe, Kuahmel, Steve Abee, Teresa Mei Chuc, Zoe Blaq, Iris Berry, A. Razor, Tanzila Ahmed, John Dorsey, Jerry the

Priest, Romus Simpson, Tares Oburumu, Adura Ojo, Francisco Escamilla aka Busstop Prophet, Erika Ayon, Steve Hochman, and supporter Susan Hayden. Anna Broome—you've given me so much support and friendship and a consistent home in the Broome Room. To Luis J. Rodriguez, Neelanjana Banerjee, Daniel A. Olivas, and Ruben J. Rodriguez for *The Coiled Serpent*; all my CS bookmates, starting with Jessica M. Wilson and Juan Cardenas and your Los Angeles Poet Society. Brendan Constantine, Peggy Dobreer, Elena Secota, Cynthia Alessandra Briano, Aruni Wijesinghe, Art Curim, Armine Iknadossian, Lida Parent Harris, A.D. Brayse, David McIntyre, Richard McDowell, Carol McArthur, Mary Torregrossa, Josette Siquieros, Michael C. Ford, Suzanne Lummis, Cynthia Toronto—a long-ago teacher who sadly left us; Wyatt Underwood, Hasan Jamal, Mona Jean Cedar, Jeff Boynton, Pogo Saito, Richard Modiano, Hilda Weiss, Wayne Lindberg, Roger Taus. To Lee Boek: we met twice and it didn't stick, but the third time it took and you put me into Storyphile and became family, ageless and timeless, old soul and eternal youth; Sophie Bouto, Mei Xian Qiu, Mello-Re Houston, Cassandra Lane, B.A. Williams, F. Douglas Brown, Joseph Rios, Alana Hinojosa, Monique Mitchell, Nicelle Davis. To Babafemi Babawale Babatunde and the Yellow House poets, including Samuel Adeyemi and Livingstone Ngoziukwu.

To my newest sub-community on the LA poetry scene: all my teachers, classmates, and friends in Community Literature Initiative (CLI), starting with Season Eight, Monday nights: Hiram Sims, visionary who conjured this program and the Sims Library of Poetry both, your sensitive, supportive, incisive critiques helped bring this book into being; Kuahmel, who recruited me into CLI, and thus without whom this book might not exist, certainly not in this form; the core group who helped so much with the extra tight-group workshopping: Flyy High of the unerring feedback; Benin Lemus, solid beautiful Buddhistic old soul; Lisbeth Coiman, whose images drip with life; Valerie Nies, surgical wit; Christina Brown, for your humor and sensitivity; to Ron Dowell, accountability partner and true, deep poet brimming over with metaphor and soul, so much respect; Recoe Walker, Morgan Danielle, James Cornelison, Soniea, Sheila Scott Head, Leve Ross, Aurea, Treesje Thomas. We went through the pandemic together and got deep into each other's work and lives before we ever even met in person, many of us: I wish you all peace, love, and poetry. James Coats, Tommy Domino. Anansi Writers Workshop. Everyone at the Sims Library of Poetry and my co-publishers at World Stage Press for giving this book birth and a home: Hiram Sims and Conney Williams; my book designer Emily Anne Evans for taking these words and designing them into a real object that I can hold in my hand; Karo Ska, Alex Petunia, Yani Davis, AKoldPiece, Camari Hawkins, V. Kali, Ruddy Lopez, everyone else.

To Lisa M. Grosso-Bosker for taking such good, loving care of my dad in his final days.

Special thanks to Kate Maruyama for your professional guidance on edits to the afterword/essay: you helped bring focus and structure to a more sprawling prior draft. A second round of thanks to Eric Sims for crucial feedback on an early draft; and to Flyy High for close reading and crucial feedback on the afterword and preface both. Thanks to Heather Pease for her contribution to the afterword. Also to the Monday night workshop folks: Lee Boek (again), Mei Xian Qiu (again), Paul Fleisher, Paul Andrade, and Erica Stewart, for close, sympathetic hearings and feedback on the preface.

What can I say? I'm a big old sloppy sentimentalist. So thank you everyone for the love, friendship, shared adventures, and moments of illumination that made me the person and poet that made this book.

And again, to everyone I've unjustly overlooked: all thanks.

At this moment, I feel made of gratitude.

About the Author

Photo by Elise Rodriguez

Jeff Rogers is a poet, writer, and performer, who fell in love with the power of words, stories, poems, and songs as a child. He grew up in Michigan college towns Kalamazoo and East Lansing. Jeff dropped out of college after his sophomore year in 1983 and drove across country to Los Angeles in quest of adventure and illumination as a struggling writer. He's been an Angeleno ever since. He worked numerous jobs, from McDonald's to mechanic's assistant; changing light bulbs in office buildings at night; bookstore manager; cab driver; temp and permanent administrative office jobs; and IT Help Desk Supervisor. He also served as president of a small union local. Since 2006, he has worked in writing, communications, and media for labor unions. His first publication was a fan letter in Marvel Comics' *The Hands of Shang Chi, Master of Kung Fu* #54, July 1977, when he was 14. As a poet, he has been published in the groundbreaking anthology *The Coiled Serpent: Poets Arising from the Cultural Quakes and Shifts of Los Angeles* and various literary journals online and in print. He has performed his own and others' work extensively around Los Angeles since his first poetry reading in 1986. From 1989 he has performed, written, directed, and produced with Gray Pony, the poetry performance and theatre troupe founded in 1988 by Christopher Natale Peditto. He's been a blogger on fierceandnerdy.com as Hippie Squared and Three Line Lunch (a daily diary in three-line poems posted each day at noon) and on beenandgoing.com as LefthandedJeff. Ironically, he also invented the word blogger in 1985 as the nonsense curse word of a two-year-old girl in the poem "Blogger Old Potatoes," but lost the contest of definitions to the one we now know. Since 2017, he's helped produce and host Drunken Masters New Works Series with the visionary publishers and community-builders at Writ Large Projects. In 1989, he co-founded an annual all-lefthanded poets' reading called Write Left.

lefthandedjeff.com | @lefthandedjeff

Made in the USA
Middletown, DE
01 May 2023

29831766R00089